Tony Trimingham arrived in S̵y̵ as a 'ten pound pom'. He settlec family and establishing himsel thirties he started a second career as a counsellor and group leader.

His life changed forever in 1996 when he discovered that his 21-year-old son Damien was dependant on heroin, and even more when Damien died of an overdose 12 months later.

After writing a letter to the *Sydney Morning Herald* about his son's death and the drug scene in Australia he found himself on a journey he never expected. Ten years later the organisation Tony founded—Family Drug Support—is a well respected and established service for families of drug and alcohol users. Tony's work has been recognised by numerous honours and awards including an Order of Australia Medal and the Prime Minister's Award for Excellence in Drug and Alcohol Endeavours.

Tony lives in the Blue Mountains with his wife Sandra and their groodles, Molly and Desmond.

To Damien—your light still shines

Not My Family Never My Child

What to do if someone you love is a drug user

Tony Trimingham

ALLEN&UNWIN

First published in 2009

Allen & Unwin
83 Alexander Street
Crows Nest NSW 2065
Australia
Phone: (61 2) 8425 0100
Fax: (61 2) 9906 2218
Email: info@allenandunwin.com
Web: www.allenandunwin.com

National Library of Australia
Cataloguing-in-Publication entry:

Trimingham, Tony.

  Not my family, never my child : what to do if someone you love is a drug user
  / Tony Trimingham.

  978 1 74175 525 1 (pbk.)

  Drug abuse–Australia. Drug addicts–Family relationships–Australia. Drug
  addiction–Australia–Prevention. Drug addiction–Treatment–Australia.

362.290994

Set in 10.5/14pt Stempel Schneidler by Midland Typesetters, Australia
Printed in Australia by McPherson's Printing Group

10 9 8 7 6 5 4 3 2 1

FSC
Mixed Sources
Product group from well-managed
forests and other controlled sources
Cert no. SGS-COC-004121
www.fsc.org
© 1996 Forest Stewardship Council

This book is printed on FSC-certified paper. The printer holds FSC
chain of custody SGS-COC-004121. The FSC promotes environmentally
responsible, socially beneficial and economically viable management of
the world's forests.

contents

foreword

by Reverend Bill Crews

I remember, over thirty years ago, Reverend Ted Noffs saying that he had buried too many kids who had died from a drug overdose. The deaths of all these kids played on his conscience, which ended up with me helping him to devise Life Education Centres.

When, in the mid-eighties, I came to Ashfield, I started a group for parents of children who had died from a drug overdose. That was one of the most painful periods of my life. At every weekly meeting a new family arrived grieving over the loss of their son or daughter. In many ways, for many years, we were so busy catering with that weekly rush of new members, we never got beyond week one of the 'therapy'. So many kids died.

For me, it was a lonely life until Tony Trimingham came along. My God, what a terrible way to meet someone. Tony's son, Damien, had recently died of a drug overdose, and he was struggling to come to terms with it. He felt that he could help parents suffering from the same situation.

Tony's story was so many parents' story. A child born with such love, hope and potential, only to die of the needle—alone and in the darkness. Yet, out of all his suffering, Tony has done so much good. Through Tony, so much help has been offered to other parents. For him, the struggle has not been easy, but when you've lost your son, what else have you got to lose? No slings, arrows, barbs or attacks from publicity-minded wowsers or politicians can ever cut like that.

I well remember the first memorial service we ran for parents of addicts who had died. Literally hundreds of people turned up. In the service, each one of us lights a candle in memory of our loved one and tears freely flow. This service has continued now for more years than I can remember and the feeling is always the same. Death by drug overdose is not something people in our society want to talk about, and so often funerals are rushed and unsatisfying. Death is a great leveller. It doesn't matter how we die, the mourning is the same. These services constantly remind me of that. We love our children because of who they are. We mightn't, at times, approve of what they do, but no matter how they die, the pain and the mourning we go through is the same and needs to be validated.

Tony's story is a story of triumph. It is one of overcoming obstacles, standing up for what you believe in and saving lives along the way.

For Tony, that can never make up for the loss, pain and suffering he went through to bring him to this point. But I do know that, 'somewhere up there', Damien is ever so proud of his dad for all that he has done, and is patiently waiting to tell him so.

introduction

My earliest memory of Tony Trimingham is of reading a most moving commentary by him in the *Sydney Morning Herald* in 1997 just after his son Damien had died from a heroin overdose. I then contacted Tony and arranged to meet him. In many ways, Damien Trimingham had lost his life to the war against drugs. The *'Just Say No'* brigade were never going to furnish the type of information or options Damien needed to help him make different decisions on the day of his death. On a number of occasions I have heard Tony re-create how Damien must have spent his last hours. This has brought many audiences to tears—all over Australia and in a number of other countries. Tony always points out that on his last journey, Damien must have walked close to the site of what has been, since 2001, the Sydney Medically Supervised Injecting Centre at Kings Cross. If Damien had injected heroin in the Medically Supervised Injecting Centre instead of the lonely basement of a building, he might well still be alive today.

By creating Family Drug Support (FDS), Tony has tried to turn a terrible negative into something positive. Tony wants other families going through what his family went through to be able to draw on the strength and rich experience of others. It is to Tony's great credit that he quickly recognised the failure and futility of the war against drugs. Tony knew, contrary to the propaganda about drug users, that his son was not bad or stupid or maladjusted or suicidal. In fact, by all accounts, Damien was a bright, interesting and insightful young man with dreams for his own future. Tony soon realised that drug policy extremism might be clever politics but that families pay for this with their blood.

Damien's death in 1997 was the result of a toxic combination of alcohol and drugs after a period of abstinence. Most drug users now understand that this is a recipe for disaster. In the eleven years since, harm minimisation strategies and a heroin shortage have ensured that deaths like Damien's are much less common. The number of deaths from heroin in Australia each year has dropped from over one thousand in 1999 to over three hundred in recent years. This is still unacceptable, but at least each year seven hundred fewer sets of boyfriends and girlfriends and mums and dads are not going to spend the rest of their lives grieving.

When I first met Tony he was struggling to understand Damien's death and trying to imagine what the political landscape might look like where someone like Damien did not die of an overdose. In finding his way, Tony looked to policy-makers and practitioners. I provided him with some advice about alcohol and drug services and policy options including harm minimisation and drug law reform, and was happy to introduce him to the community of people wanting a better way. Perhaps Tony saw me initially as part of the status quo, the system that had seen his son die, and was keen to make his own way rather than 'hitch a wagon'. Still, he could see the sense of harm minimisation, recognised the steps already taken, and quickly began to work out his own position.

Harm minimisation is based on the understanding that drug dependence is often a relapsing condition and that caring for drug users must focus first and foremost on keeping them alive. After all, where there is life, there is hope. Sometimes keeping drug users alive necessitates methods that might seem counter-intuitive, like providing sterile injection equipment and safer places to inject, replacing (street) drugs with similar (controlled) drugs, and distributing honest information to users about drugs, vein care, blood-borne viruses and drug management. This approach can be baffling for parents, who want their child simply to stop taking drugs and stay clean. They find it hard to accept the need to provide their child with the means to inject their drugs less dangerously, when all they want to do is put a match to all drugs and all drug paraphernalia on Planet Earth.

Harm minimisation could not have become such a force in Australia without the support of the families of users. Tony Trimingham took the lead in assisting families to understand that harm minimisation represents the best chance of keeping their son, daughter, sibling or parent alive—alive to seek treatment, to enjoy remission, to survive relapse. Tony then reflected this view of drug users as a representative of families to politicians and practitioners: we may hate what they do, but we will always love who they are, and we demand a respectful, intelligent and therapeutic approach to managing alcohol and drug problems.

Tony drew his strength from the families of other users, and in doing so made a major contribution to Australian drug policy. He formed an identifiable and powerful political coalition, pulling families onto centre stage in the great drug debate. For the first time in Australia there was a confluence between those affected at the most personal and heartfelt level, and those treating users and trying to develop a more effective, more evidence-based and more compassionate public health policy. The importance of this cannot be understated, in terms of empowering families, enriching the debate and turning the tide of public opinion.

FDS grew out of this coalition, nurtured carefully by Tony's wide research and good sense. FDS provided a bridge for families to appropriate alcohol and drug service providers and into the policy process. Most importantly, Tony has ensured a focus on what is realistic and achievable. FDS has helped families understand the relapsing nature of addiction and encouraged them to accept the reality of their situation. FDS fosters an *eyes wide open* approach where there is always room for the positive.

It has been my experience as a clinician that family support is often a primary factor in promoting less destructive behaviour and improving the chances of remission for drug users. FDS, under Tony's stewardship, has helped to heal many relationships. The FDS philosophy recognises that when families take care of their own emotional and health needs and gain new skills, relationships with drug-using members need not be inflexible or ever diminishing. Families are encouraged to support but not rescue, to accept but not approve, to develop boundaries, to learn from past experiences, and to help each other through FDS meetings.

I am pleased that Tony's story is finally being told in full. Many people will identify with it, and most readers, connecting with the personal tragedy, will see the good sense that drug law reform represents and the heartache that it can stop. Things must change, for all the 'Damiens' in Australia and for all the 'Tonys' too.

Families, users themselves and those involved in alcohol and drug treatment are the better for Tony's contribution. But this is just the catalyst. There is so much more to do, to make sure that Damien's death truly becomes a focus for positive change, until we are at a point where we say: 'Remember when people used to die of drug overdose, of blood-borne viruses? Remember the stigma and loss of dignity? It seems so hard to believe that we humans could ever have let that happen to one of our own . . .'

The decision on 19 August 1997 by Federal Cabinet, in reality by the then prime minister John Howard, to abort a rigorous scientific prescription heroin trial despite a recent 6:3 vote of national Health and Police and Justice ministers, marked the beginnings of a new era. Three months later Howard announced his *'Tough on Drugs'* policy, though fortunately policy rarely matched the harsh rhetoric and was mainly just a political strategy. Tony played a critical national role in the following years, speaking out for the families who had lost their own children to the war against drugs. Tony knew from his own experience that this was really the *war against drug users*. Now, a little more than a decade later, we have evidence from research in Switzerland, the Netherlands, Germany, Spain and Canada showing clearly that prescription heroin treatment benefits severe heroin users who have not previously benefited from any other treatment. If the treatment of drug users is to improve like the treatment of heart disease, diabetes or cancer, we need quality scientific research free of political interference.

In the months leading up to May 1999, Tony and I were part of a group of about a dozen people who established the 'Tolerance Room' in the basement of the Wayside Chapel in Sydney's Kings Cross. This was Australia's first Medically Supervised Injecting Centre. The project was denounced by the then prime minister John Howard, even before it had opened its doors. The 'Tolerance Room' was a civil disobedience project intended to encourage the NSW government to have the fortitude to accept a Wood Royal Commission recommendation to establish a sanctioned Injecting Centre. Despite being raided by the police on three occasions, the 'Tolerance Room' persisted long enough for the NSW government to agree to refer the issue to the 1999 NSW Drug Summit. A clear majority at the Drug Summit supported the establishment of an official Medically Supervised Injecting Centre.

Tony's life has been changed irrevocably by Damien's death. He now travels a great deal and is a national identity. He has been invited to join prestigious committees and give talks to distinguished audiences. Tony's name is regularly in the newspapers and his dry Cumbrian accent can often be heard rasping away on radio or television. I have heard Tony say many times that he would gladly give all of this up to be reunited with Damien, even momentarily. I have no doubt he is telling us the absolute truth. He is reminding us that human life is sacred, and that our politicians have let us down by selling us policies they know themselves to have failed egregiously, again and again.

Nothing lasts forever. Until 1953, doctors could lawfully prescribe heroin in Australia. Australia's heroin problems started some years after heroin was prohibited, not before. At some time in the future, the community will force our politicians to accept that drugs regulated by criminals and corrupt police are even more dangerous than drugs regulated by authorities. Tony Trimingham has made a huge contribution to finding more effective, more evidence-based and more compassionate ways of responding to illicit drugs, and he has done that by tapping the immense resources of wisdom in the community.

Dr Alex Wodak, Director,
Alcohol and Drug Service,
St Vincent's Hospital, Sydney
29 January 2008

Acknowledgements

Obviously our staff are a vital ingredient of the future of Family Drug Support (FDS), so to Fay, to Tricia, to Sandra—a huge and heartfelt thanks. Their commitment is far beyond that of normal workers and, as my wife, Sandra also provides me with invaluable emotional support—something that she has done with love and compassion since my son Damien died. People at the coalface of FDS include Kath Ashton in South Australia—another amazing woman who works far beyond any expectations—and Theo and Antonia, who I believe are the future of FDS. They have tremendous skills and enormous compassion and they are out there pushing our philosophies and the support that we give to families—heartfelt thanks to them.

Pam, Jim, Linda, Margaret and Hera also deserve a huge thank you—as do so many other of our wonderfully dedicated facilitators.

Our marvellous Helpline volunteers are the lifeblood of FDS—too many people to mention here, but they know who they are and should also know that they do contribute so much and so positively. Thank you—all of you—for putting in so much time and energy beyond the usual volunteer workload.

I would also like to make a special mention of all the people—some of whom are valued FDS staff members and volunteers—who showed the courage to share their personal stories for this book. I am sure that their own tales of living with someone who is drug-dependent will help others on their own difficult journey.

Various board members of FDS over the years have been incredibly important. When we first started, the board consisted, almost exclusively, of affected family members, and without their energy and determination we couldn't have got going and achieved all that we have today.

Ann Symonds, our first chair, really gave us some direction and took us places we never expected to go, and then, of late, Professor Peter Baume has continued that. As we move into the future, the board is becoming more skilled but still retains those elements of family that are so important to FDS.

More thanks to our professional panel who back us up with their expertise and skills. They have provided FDS with that professional edge so needed that has helped us review our resources along the way, and their belief in what we do has been invaluable.

Thanks to Brian and Marion McConnell who lost their son to heroin and helped start an organisation, Family and Friends for Drug Law Reform. They are tireless campaigners for more human drug strategies.

There have also been some really good friends on all sides of politics. On the state side I would single out John Della Bosca and also Robert Oakeshott, who left the National Party and admitted that the worst day of his life was when he was forced to vote against the injecting centre as a member of the Nationals. Bob Carr was always very supportive of everything we did too, as was Linda Burney, and John Ryan from the Liberal Party was also very positive about our work. On a federal level, ALP parliamentarian Tanya Plibersek has been a strong supporter, while on the Liberal side of things Brendan Nelson, Marise Payne and John Brogden have also been supportive.

One person I have always had very high regard for is Professor Margaret Hamilton. During my time on the Australian National Council on Drugs (ANCD), she sort of took me under her wing. I have been patronised by some experts over the years but never by her. The tireless Dr Alek Wodak has also been both inspiration and support over the years and I thank him for his belief in the work FDS does.

I also acknowledge Claire Halliday without whom the book would not have been written.

An organisation like FDS can only be sustained by collective wisdom and strength, and so to anyone I have missed out, my deepest thanks and appreciation. I truly believe that we can make a difference—but we need to work together. I hope that we can all continue to do so in the future.

AMBIVALENCE
by Damien Trimingham

Embroiled in a drug-filled haze
Melting defence got lost in the maze
Lost to my own desire to hurt
Lost to the girl and a white-powdered dirt
Confused the emotion of pleasure and pain
Playing my life like playing a game
Caught in my own self-spinning web
Fighting a war that exists in my head
The inner child has lost to the man
That couldn't see past an indifferent plan
Lost every rational thought in my head
Caught in a shell with nothing but time
And now as I watch yet I'm shielding my eyes
With a needle protruding I'm feeding the lies
A memory, a thought, a relinquishing sigh
A decision to live or to die
'To be or to be not' said the guilt-ridden Dane
To find out the truth and finish the game
Watching the screen now my battle's been won
But what of the kids whose battles go on?
Understand, educate and never be blind
To a drug that steals health, spirit and mind.

CHAPTER 1

After the First Death

In those first moments of your baby's new life, so many things come to mind. You look at their tiny toenails and eyelashes and marvel at the absolute perfectness of something so very small and fragile. You look at their face and squirming body and recognise glimpses of yourself, and then you wonder what the future will bring—whether they will make the mistakes you did, whether they will go on to be prime minister, or simply happy, or, one day, perhaps, the father of their own, equally perfect baby son.

In those first moments of your baby's new life, amid all the excitement and anticipation of what may come in the days and years to follow, you never imagine anything bad. You don't let your mind wander to thoughts of danger or destruction, and you never, ever imagine that brand-new child's death.

Twenty-three years after my own joyful delivery-room dreams, though, that perfect baby—my son—did die. Damien's life ended in an empty stairwell of St Margaret's Hospital, Surry Hills—the place where my dreams for him had begun just a couple of decades before. He was discovered by a security guard on night patrol—obviously in trouble, having overdosed on heroin. By the time the guard followed his company's official procedure and called for back-up, Damien was dead.

Damien was 23 when he died. He was white, Anglo-Saxon, and I guess what could be described as middle class. But he could have been female, 14 or 40, black, Asian or European, from a poor or rich family, from Toorak, Dubbo, Alice Springs or Cabramatta. For drugs, as I had already discovered, do not discriminate.

Damien was a talented person. During his time at school, he was a state champion athlete, elite footballer, school prefect, house captain, actor, poet and musician. He was loved by all his friends—and their parents. He was, at times, a person who lived close to the edge—he was certainly fearless on the football field. In eras gone by, I would not be surprised if he would have been first in line to enlist for battle to take that bravado headfirst into the unknown, without fear of the possible consequences. I later found this is common with many drug users—they are often artistic, creative, scientific and fearless.

Hand-in-hand with his many fine qualities, Damien was certainly no angel, often getting into strife in his adolescence. The first substances he used were alcohol and tobacco—like many Australians these were sampled while he was just a young teenager—and, in addition, he also dabbled with cannabis.

Since leaving Chatswood High in 1992, he had worked in a stable job as manager of a service station, and his girlfriend of three years was employed as a hairdresser. He had an active social life and many friends. Life for him, I thought, was good. I didn't know he had been hiding a secret.

Damien had often expressed his negativity to hard drugs, and so when I saw signs that caused concern—change in eating and sleeping habits, constant lack of money, niggling health problems—and questioned him, his 'Don't be stupid, Dad—do you think I'm crazy?' made sense, and I breathed a sigh of relief. What I didn't know, until June 1996, was that he had, over a period of eight months or more, developed a severe heroin habit.

When I finally found out about the reality of his life, I discovered that he and his girlfriend had been using about $600 worth of heroin a day. They had gone through their combined savings and spent a total of $30000 on heroin, sold all their property of value and borrowed extensively from friends and strangers. They had stopped paying their rent and bills, and I believe they were probably one step away from crime when Damien's girlfriend's father discovered their debts and confronted them. I returned from a trip to England with my partner Sandra to find Damien on my doorstep with a very sad and sorry tale.

Like most parents, I was totally unprepared and unable to deal with the news. As Damien told me, I just went numb. After listening for about ten minutes I had to walk into another room. I became overwhelmed with emotions. There was instant guilt and blame—why has this happened to me? To my son? To my family? What had we done wrong? Was it because I had got divorced twice? Twenty years as a counsellor and I hadn't seen it coming? I talked with my son about everything. How had I missed it?

Then there was fear. I realised immediately that I knew so little about drugs—especially heroin. I knew people died. Was Damien going to die?

Grief was another raging emotion. In that one conversation, all my hopes, dreams and aspirations for Damien went out of the window. He had lost everything . . . and so had I.

I went back into the room where Damien was sobbing, and these emotions quickly evaporated, only to be replaced with the type of emotion so many dads are very good at—anger. I let him have it: how stupid he was, how selfish he was, how much he had let me down.

After a while, everything drained away. I collapsed in a chair. Then I dragged myself out of the chair, grabbed my son by the collar and again did what most fathers do in these circumstances—I set about trying to fix it. Men are, after all, problem-solvers. My words to him were, 'We are going to beat this, son.' I had no idea how difficult that would be.

I tried to contact services I believed would offer me help and support, but found that for the families of drug users there really wasn't any help or support available. When I rang treatment services, desperate to find help I thought would see Damien get better, the first response was, 'How old is he?' Not 'How is he?' or 'How are you?' As soon as I told them he was 22 they said, 'Sorry, can't talk to you.' Now, I kind of understand that he had to be the one to make the moves to fix his own life, but at the time it felt very heartless. There was no one trying to engage with the family at all, and with the shame and stigma of the situation so obvious all around us, we did what most people do—we kept it to ourselves.

My solution was to pack Damien off to my daughter Gillian's place in the Blue Mountains—naïvely thinking that if he could just get away from his usual crowd of friends and dealers, he would be okay. I had no idea what I was putting Gillian through, but somehow she and Damien managed to survive his cold-turkey withdrawal. All the while, I was back home in Sydney, working my way through all the normal but, in hindsight, very negative coping strategies—denial, anger and self-blame.

My secondary denial came shortly after—when I thought that, because he had stopped using, most of the danger was gone. I have since found out that it is a common reaction for families to find themselves in this situation and think that their problems are over. At the time, though, I didn't realise how wrong I was.

For the next eight months Damien was largely drug-free, occasionally drinking heavily and weighed down with guilt and a sense of failure. He felt that he'd lost all his friends. He had lost his girlfriend and there was the feeling that he had let his family and himself down. In between these times of despairing reflection, there were also times of optimism—he started mountain climbing, took up rugby training and even developed a new relationship. He had a happy-go-lucky optimistic personality and this often endeared him to people—even through his struggle.

It was an emotional rollercoaster but, still, I thought that he was on the road to recovery. I discovered later—only after his death, when I was able to read his personal diary and journal—that in the bad times he would return to the comfort of drugs, take off for the city, score some heroin, use it in a back alley or toilet block, sleep it off, and then return to the Blue Mountains. It was while he was on one of these trips, in February 1997, that he died.

He'd had an argument with his girlfriend, then a heavy drinking session, withdrew his last $50 from an ATM and caught the 7.30 p.m. train from Katoomba. Damien got off at Central Station, walked to Bourke Street Pharmacy at Taylor Square and bought the needle 'fits' he needed to inject. In an average week at that time, over ten years ago, this particular pharmacy sold over 8000 syringes. The week of my son's death—which was Mardi Gras week—they had sold over 15 000.

In the eyes of the police officer who would eventually ring me, three days after my son had been found, to tell me of his death, Damien was just another junkie. The same was true of the morgue workers I met. At that time in Australia, three or four families a day were experiencing a similar heartbreak.

By the time I went to make the formal identification of Damien's body at the Glebe Morgue, the autopsy had already been performed—his internal organs removed, weighed and measured with no regard for the life they had once been a part of. Twelve months later, I found out that those organs—perfectly healthy, according to the coroner's report—had been sent to Sydney University for medical research. They were never returned to us. To so many people, Damien was just another dead body. To me, he was my irreplaceable boy—that perfect baby son. Life would never be the same again.

Four hundred, mostly young people came to Damien's funeral and told stories about a charming, charismatic, creative young man who had once had so many reasons to live. After celebrating his life, most people returned to their own normal lives, and Damien became a memory—someone to be looked back upon occasionally, while they continued to move forward.

For his family, there was no moving forward—just the shattered pieces of a life we once knew. In my case, given the nature of his death and the fact that it was so preventable, I was also left with a lot of anger.

That anger was initially directed at the dealers who had sold my boy the drugs that were his downfall. I gave all the mobile-phone numbers from Damien's phone to the local police, and then my anger moved to the next target—the government. It began to consume me.

Grief has a way of making you feel that you are the only one suffering, but I soon realised that what had been such a shocking death for me and my family was far from an isolated incident. All over Australia, other fathers, other mothers, other brothers and other sisters were feeling that pain. For me, the added pain comes from knowing that so many more are yet to feel it. Because still to this day, drugs don't discriminate.

CHAPTER 2

The Big Picture

What other country boasts of a former prime minister who was, at one time, one of the world's fastest drinkers? Before the *Guinness Book of Records* banned all alcohol-related entries in 1991 (for fear, I suppose, of any litigation from people risking alcohol poisoning in the name of similar notoriety), our very own prime minister Robert (Bob) Hawke was listed, back in 1955 and while on a Rhodes Scholarship to Oxford University, as drinking 2.5 pints of beer in just eleven seconds. In his 1994 book, *The Hawke Memoirs*, he wrote: 'this feat was to endear me to some of my fellow Australians more than anything else I ever achieved'.

Most countries in the world have substance-abuse problems, but the exact nature of the problems and the type of drugs used vary from country to country. And while each country has its own way of dealing with drug users, no country has eliminated drug problems—even countries where zero tolerance is enforced. We often hear comments that Australia should adopt this or that overseas strategy; however, it is arguable which countries actually have the best, most effective approaches. While overseas research and experience is important, and some aspects of some strategies may assist in our own backyard, it is vital that we understand the unique elements of Australian drug culture.

Moderation is not really the Australian way, and ours is a culture which has prided itself on being a nation of larrikins— founded by convicts and with a history that has encouraged and celebrated both rebellion and risk-taking. Our national heroes include rebels, bushrangers and others who bend the rules to near breaking point—Ned Kelly, Breaker Morant, Shane Warne and Brett Whiteley. Examples of our sporting icons hit the headlines regularly for their dalliances with drugs or alcohol excess, and a glance at the weekly women's magazines shows that we happily absorb the 'famous for fifteen minutes' cult of celebrity heroes and heroines who are in and out of rehab as quickly as they change their designer outfits.

At the same time, a small but vocal, right-leaning moral and religious aspect of our society, combined with Australia's increasingly expanding diversity and multiculturalism, has also had an impact on community attitudes to drugs and drug-taking. While certain sectors of the Australian community take to bingeing (excessive consumption of drugs or alcohol), other voices promote abstinence as the only way.

As has been reported widely in all media outlets in recent times, bingeing—especially among young and even underage people—is an extreme concern. Unfortunately, in many social groups—both younger and older—this is still accepted as appropriate behaviour and part of what makes us Aussies.

Poly drug use (mixing combinations of more than one drug) is also alarmingly common. At private parties, music festivals and nightclubs across the country, many people consume drugs such as ecstasy, alcohol, marijuana, amphetamines or prescription drugs, without considering how these drugs will act when combined in the body. The experiment can be disastrous—even fatal.

Add to that the fact that heroin, whether originating from South-East Asia or, increasingly, from Afghanistan, continues to be a very big problem—robbing young Australians of their true potential and, sometimes, their lives.

But Australia's biggest drug problem—alcohol—is not about furtive alleyway deals and illegal importation. What it means to be Australian has gone hand-in-hand with alcohol consumption for generations, and today the alcohol industry continues to market beverages towards younger and younger drinkers. Alcohol-related problems are increasing, particularly since the advent of alcopops—those fizzy, lolly-coloured drinks that have flooded the alcohol market and attracted the attention of our young Australians.

More recently, we have seen the introduction of alcoholic drinks containing guarana and other naturally derived stimulants, which are also attractive to the youth market, given the fact that, in the past, these additives have been more at home in 'sports' and 'energy' drinks.

Statistics, both here and internationally, show that teenagers who smoke and drink in early teen years are more inclined to try other drugs than teenagers who abstain. Some people, in fact, refer to alcohol and tobacco as the 'gateway' drugs. The reason? Although these same experts acknowledge that there are, of course, many, many people who smoke tobacco and/or drink alcohol who have never tried anything stronger, it is believed that by exhibiting some risk-taking behaviour (we all know that the links between smoking tobacco and various diseases are real), taking yet another step towards even riskier behaviour, such as smoking marijuana, might seem less of a leap. There is also evidence to suggest that teenagers are more likely to smoke and drink heavily if their parents do. Finally the community is taking notice but alcohol use is concerning and it is time to curb the excess.

Over 3000 Australians die each year as a result of harmful drinking. Data from the National Drug Strategy Household Survey (2007) indicates that over 80 per cent of the population consumed alcohol in the previous twelve months, with 11 per cent of males and 6 per cent of females drinking daily. In Australia, alcohol misuse costs the Australian community over seven billion dollars each year, including 1.2 billion dollars in crime. Over 230 000 children (13.2 per cent) live in households where they are at risk of exposure to binge-drinking by at least one adult. In Indigenous Aboriginal communities across the country, these figures are even higher.

Current affairs programs and radio shock jocks may harp on about 'the war on drugs', but it is alcohol, I believe, that, more than any other drug, represents the most serious threat to public safety. Not only does it have a direct effect on the health of your mind and body, alcohol use also increases the risks associated with driving and is involved in a significantly high number of road accidents, drownings, sexual assaults and other crimes of violence, arrests, unsafe sex practices and other high-risk behaviour that can include even further drug experimentation.

In March 2008 I was pleased to see that Prime Minister Kevin Rudd announced a $53 million plan to tackle binge-drinking—focusing heavily on sporting clubs and the influence they can have on the lives of impressionable young people in the community. The subsequent campaign—featuring prominent sporting identities warning of the dangers of binge-drinking—seemed like a good start, but it's difficult to treat such an advertising campaign too seriously when, at the same time, alcohol companies are allowed to pump millions of dollars into sponsorship of high-profile sporting events.

The rise of 'schoolies culture'—a phenomenon that has, in the past decade, seen tens of thousands of secondary school students flood coastal hot spots from Victoria to the Gold Coast for week-long, post-exam celebrations—is also of enormous concern, and says a lot about our society's 'party hard and drink till you drop' mentality, which seems to be flourishing, particularly in the minds of the younger generation.

It's time the community rallied against this greedy lack of responsibility shown by the alcohol companies, and time that governments also stood up for our young people—putting their lives above any associated tax benefits that come from the sales of such drinks. Yes, parents need to model responsible drinking; yes, young people need to be more aware of alcohol and its effects; but, more than anything, we need to say 'enough is enough' to the industry and its pressures. Our young people already experience so many other areas of concern, such as depression, unemployment and mental illness—all of which may coincide with problematic drug or alcohol use that only serves to exacerbate existing or underlying conditions, rather than ease them.

Today, more and more young Australians are being diagnosed with mental-health issues and thousands more go undiagnosed. The Australian Bureau of Statistics reported in 1999 that one in five people in Australia will suffer from a mental illness of some kind within their lifetime. The most common of these are anxiety, depression and psychosis. The last ten years in Australia have seen significant advancements in the knowledge and evidence about such issues, and we now know that there is a strong link between mental-health disorders and regular or dependent drug or alcohol use. The Australian Bureau of Statistics found in both 1999 and 2006 that a higher prevalence of substance use among people with mental-health issues was commonly reported nationally.

For some, drug use is a stage (chaotic and traumatic for families at the time) which they get over and leave behind. Others, however, can get stuck in dependency and may develop long-term, more deeply entrenched problems. Illicit drug use is associated with over 1000 deaths per year in Australia, typically among young people. And while statistics often show that two-thirds of drug users are males, it is clear that young females are catching up—and fast.

When it comes to marijuana, there is mixed evidence and ongoing debate regarding its associated risks. Over the years, it has been used by hundreds of thousands of Australians and, like alcohol, does not cause major problems for the majority of those who try it. Like alcohol, though, those who do get into trouble as a result of using it often experience great distress and the families who call our helpline would certainly not see it as a benign drug.

Marijuana users from the 1960s still remember a gentle high, ingested through smoking a joint, mostly consisting of the less powerful leafy part of the marijuana plant, today's smokers typically inhale the more potent 'heads' or 'buds' of the plant, often through bongs or pipes that give a more concentrated, intense hit of smoke. Many experts believe that, because marijuana smoked in bongs or pipes is usually mixed with tobacco, part of the craving for the drug comes from the addiction to nicotine. Even though there is still no firm evidence that marijuana causes mental illness, most experts agree that marijuana can trigger underlying conditions from depression through to schizophrenia.

I have a 22-year-old son, James, who has Asperger's syndrome—a 'high functioning' form of autism. James started using marijuana several years ago, which only exacerbated the situation and caused some severe behavioural problems. Now that James has given up marijuana those issues have resolved themselves.

With the decline in heroin use from 2000 onwards, we have, unfortunately, seen a growth in Australia of stimulants—ecstasy, cocaine, and particularly speed and 'ice', aka crystal methamphetamine. But whether it is marijuana, alcohol, speed, heroin or prescription drugs, I do think that we should not get too caught up in media-driven frenzies about which drug is 'the scourge of society' this week or next. While it is true that the range of drugs on offer has widened more than ever before to include opiates, barbiturates and amphetamines, and the nature of drug users and their resulting drain on law enforcement and health services has also changed for the worse, the individual drug causing the problem shouldn't really matter. It is the individual behind it that needs the help of the community. And behind that individual stands their family—confused, saddened, worried sick and, often, without the adequate support to help them cope.

Despite the prevalence of drugs in Australia, communities still tend to see drugs as 'someone else's problem' or, sometimes, a 'teenage problem' that kids will grow out of before any real damage is done. Nothing really prepares us for the realisation that it may be happening to our family, and even when we do become aware of it, we often deny what's happening. It's certainly not something we regularly discuss with our neighbours, friends and work colleagues.

It's time to speak out more. By opening up a dialogue about this issue—in the home and as part of education in the school system—we will get the message across, where and when it really matters.

Since Damien died, I have realised how at-risk our young people are. It's a vulnerability that I see regularly, as I tour schools across the country—taking my message to secondary students in the hope that they won't make the same choices my son did. Education is, I believe, one effective way to turn that faint hope into a more positive reality for the future.

At the start of my talk, I ask the assembled teenage audience to stand, then ask them to sit down if they have used various substances. Around 85 per cent sit down when I say 'alcohol'. I call out the names of other drugs that are both legal and illicit and I watch as, one by one, most of the children—some as young as thirteen—take their seats. Usually, none are left standing.

Our young people are taking drugs. They are drinking alcohol. In order to try to fight this statistic, we need to start talking about the issue of drugs and alcohol openly and honestly, in an effort to come up with real-world approaches and solutions. Telling them not to do it hasn't worked. Back in the early days of the twentieth century, prohibition didn't work for alcohol, and it doesn't work now for other drugs. Educating our young people about how to live with drugs and alcohol in the safest way possible will lead to change. By offering this education, it doesn't mean that their behaviour in terms of drug or alcohol use is being sanctioned. It is a message of warning, wrapped up in the sensible reality that, for some, an outright warning just won't be enough. For those young people—the ones who will experiment—I hope that they will do so more cautiously and with a better understanding of the possible ramifications . . . not just for them but for all those who love and spend time with them.

When I start my presentation with a slide show of my son as a happy, smiling baby, the young audience recognises some part of themselves in the family photos that have been taken at sports events and birthday parties, I know that I am making an emotional connection. I see them thinking 'this could be me'.

Then the final photos of Damien appear on the screen and that recognition turns to shock. If they have seen a part of themselves in his journey, it is clear that, at least in the darkness of their school auditorium, they don't want that journey to end as his did—undignified and alone, being photographed for part of an official police report on his death in a dark stairwell. Just another drug-death statistic.

Our drug problem in Australia is complex and multi-faceted but I do believe it can be changed. It will take the work of individuals armed with the right knowledge; it will take the work of communities to support those individuals; and it will take the work of governments to support those communities. It cannot be done alone. But I believe it can be done. It may also need some realistic and courageous law reform.

Although most young people will not die or even have major problems, this has gone too far to ignore any longer. The next drug or alcohol statistic could be your son, your daughter, your brother, sister or parent. It is already too late for me. Don't let it be too late for you.

CHAPTER 3

No, You Are Not Alone—Family Drug Support

Damien's experience as a drug user opened my eyes to a world I had never fully understood. I guess that's what happens to a lot of people who go through any sudden shock or trauma—you never know what it's really like until it happens to you.

When it came to drugs, I had, I suppose, been much the same as many other Australians—I read the occasional drug-related horror story in the papers, I watched the occasional news reports highlighting the latest drug scourge to hit our streets, but I never really felt motivated to have a strong opinion either way about what should or shouldn't be done to rectify the problem. If anything, I think I probably had a hard-line/don't-care approach.

The day Damien came to tell me that he was using drugs, that all changed. Not immediately, admittedly—there was the bluster of my parental anger and frustration to sort through first. However, once those initial feelings of fear, anger and confusion had subsided, my next instinct was to seek whatever help might be available for both my son and myself, and I realised so many things needed to change.

When something tragic happens to you, there is a tendency to feel as though you are all alone with your unique grief—that nobody could possibly understand what you are going through and that there is no way you will ever feel hope again. I certainly felt that way in the time after Damien's death. About six months into my initial, desperate grief—a time when I was sinking into depression and merely going through the motions of living—Justice James Wood handed down the findings of his Royal Commission into police corruption, paedophilia and drugs in NSW and I could not believe the reaction.

For politicians on both sides, his recommendations regarding heroin, such as safe injecting rooms and heroin trials, all seemed just too difficult—something that made me increasingly frustrated.

At around the same time, the ACT government's proposed trial of prescription heroin to dependent users was vetoed by John Howard—even though all the state and territory Health and Justice ministers, plus Dr Michael Wooldridge—the federal minister—had agreed to it.

My personal and professional life is dotted with examples of the way I tend to use my own personal setbacks to try to do some good—either for myself or the broader community. I guess it's my way of coping. Back in 1979, when my first wife left and I was caring for our two children, I looked around for help and support and, as a result of working through my own divorce, I started training as a counsellor—trying to provide for other people what I had felt was lacking for myself. I have now been a group leader, counsellor and trainer for nearly thirty years.

When I had a very negative experience with a dating service, a couple of friends and myself started what was then Australia's first computer dating service as well as a very big singles club in Sydney. I have always tried to use life's negative experiences for positive outcomes.

So, when Damien died—after months spent trying to access proper help for both him and myself—I knew that I needed to do something to help other family members affected by the drug use of their loved one, to ensure that Damien's death had not been in vain.

To lose a child to an early death is devastating—to find that the death was totally preventable is tragic. On top of this, to realise that, in the eyes of the law and our society, he died a criminal, is heartbreak beyond belief. Each day—including today—many Australian families will also go through this kind of heartbreak.

One evening, after listening to yet another politician ducking and weaving, I couldn't sleep. I got up at three in the morning and wrote a letter to the *Sydney Morning Herald*—my impassioned plea, as a father, that my son be remembered as more than just another drug-death statistic. As a result of the subsequent publicity and interest, I was asked to write a column about Damien. It was published on May 26, 1997.

> On February 24, my 23-year-old son died in the car park of St Margaret's Hospital, Surry Hills. He lay dead in the morgue at Glebe for three days before we were notified, by telephone, of his death. A needle was still in his arm—he had been drinking heavily

through the day. Another drug-ridden no-hoper using taxpayers' money to fund a sordid habit that ended his life suddenly. For the police and mortuary workers, he was just another statistic. Twenty years ago, this incident would have been headlines in the newspaper—now it was just one of many similar deaths.

Five days later, more than 300 people met at St Stephen's Church, Willoughby to say goodbye to someone they loved. Without exceptions, they spoke of a fine young man with qualities such as cheerfulness, courtesy, courage, leadership and caring. They spoke of his sporting achievements—state champion athlete in several disciplines, champion rugby union and league player with potential for international representation. They spoke of his acting and musical talent and his poetry and his ability to reach and touch his friends with deep-seated love, they sobbed, they got angry, they talked of it being 'a good funeral'.

Damien was my son. I loved him deeply and I miss him terribly. His death was an accident, the result of deadly experimentation at a time when he was in despair. He had recently lost his long-term relationship and his job of three and a half years. Having read his personal papers, I've discovered his dark, despairing side hidden from most but fed by fantasy and black lyrics from so-called 'heroes' of this generation's music. Damien's poetry is very talented, but it reflects a hopelessness that is at the core of this generation.

I also believe that, with maturity and some success, which Damien with his talents and qualities was bound to achieve, he would have survived. He was occasionally using heroin but was not an addict; it was his escape from his despair. Everyone who works at the coal face—police, mortuary workers, social workers and counsellors—tell me that Damien should not and need not have died. They tell me that half the crime in Australia could disappear overnight. How? Their solution—full legalisation and decriminalisation of heroin use, with governments and health workers totally controlling its use and output.

Since Damien died, I have learnt a great deal about the drug culture and trade. As tragic as his death has been, his death is not the greatest tragedy. I have discovered that as many as 30 per cent of young people have experimented or are experimenting with heroin. All drug education has failed miserably.

The scum who grow rich on the deaths of this generation are allowed to go free to feed on the despair, fantasies and rebelliousness of our young people. The police didn't even want to know the name of Damien's dealer, saying they were powerless to touch him.

If someone with great courage doesn't take a risk to make radical changes, in 10 years the cost on this generation will be immense. If the public doesn't stop seeing drug addicts as a separate society deserving no sympathy or help, then their children and friends will be the next victims.

My plea, in the name of my son, Damien, who was always a leader, is to listen to Justice Wood and the Rev Bill Crews and all the men and women who pick up dead children from the streets, and try something new.

The article struck a chord and, soon after, with yet more media interest and our story being told in the TV show *Witness*, my phone started ringing and didn't stop for a week. Letters from parents were forwarded on to me from the television station. Most of the phone calls and letters were from family members of drug users—people who, like me, had seen their lives turned upside down as a result of their loved one's drug use.

One of the first people who contacted me was the only child of the great Doc Evatt (Dr Herbert Vere Evatt was one of Australia's most influential Labor leaders). She shared with me the fact that her nineteen-year-old daughter had died some years earlier from a heroin overdose. Others talked of the shame and stigma—one woman from Queensland had lost three children to drugs.

The common thing about these phone calls was that these were decent people from all walks of life who had done their best in dealing with drug use. There were common themes: no immediately available detox beds or rehabilitation places; lack of support and even discounting of families by professionals; lack of strategies for coping with all of the complex issues surrounding the drug use.

One woman from a small country town rang about the recent death of her sixteen-year-old daughter. She talked about her isolation and grief, and the relentless local gossip—her daughter was a prostitute, she'd been murdered—all totally untrue. The woman had become agoraphobic because of her fear of confronting her uncaring community. She was also angry that another family in the town who had lost a child in a rail accident had received emotional and financial support from that same community who had shunned her.

At the suggestion of Rev Bill Crews from Ashfield Uniting Church, a man with a history of ministering to minorities,

I advertised a public meeting at his church—450 people came and Family Drug Support (FDS) was formed.

Not only did we start an advocacy campaign for families—writing to newspapers and politicians, educating the community, fighting for the rights of users and their families—but we also decided to try to address some of the gaps that families were identifying as needing to be filled. We had no money and no real idea about how to run an organisation, but we were sustained by the need and the energy of our members and volunteers.

Who and what is a family?

We regard family as anyone who cares about a drug user. While most of our callers are parents roughly 40 per cent of calls are from siblings, children, relatives, friends and lovers. Not only do these different family members have different personal needs and attitudes regarding the drug use—they also present a range of issues for the parents and drug user to address.

Let's examine each of the family members and their common responses:

Children

While numbers of children accessing the FDS service regarding drug-using parents are relatively low there is no question that more children of drug users are going to need care and support in the years ahead. We have already seen the establishment of special services to assist children (Mirabel Foundation www.mirabelfoundation.com and Kids Helpline www.kidshelp.com.au or 1800 551 800).

Having to be a carer for a parent, while coping with the stresses of childhood or teenage years, is very difficult. For various reasons, young people tend not to use telephone helplines and so web-based services like Youth Drug Support (www.yds.org.au) become very important. Young people do need someone to confide in and do need a break from caring, as well as needing to have lives of their own. It is really important that they do not become isolated and cut off from help—especially when they feel that their family is not 'normal'. Other extended family members need to be in tune with what is happening and give additional support to these children.

Parents of drug users with other children

When siblings of drug users share the same house, there are many dilemmas for the parents to face— especially if the other children are much younger. It is important that children's rights and needs are being met and sometimes, with the family's emphasis on dealing with the crisis of drug-using, the problems of other siblings can be overlooked.

In the case of siblings, a direct and open communication is usually the best way of dealing with the issues, even though it can be uncomfortable. Some siblings may be sympathetic and supportive to the drug user, others may be antagonistic and critical. These feelings can also flow on to their attitude about the efforts of their parents. It is important to acknowledge that you have heard and listened to the thoughts and feelings of your other children, even if there are disagreements about how to deal with the issues. Even small children are better off knowing what is happening, rather than being isolated from reality.

Grandparents and other older relatives

Many grandparents who contact our line are concerned about their grandchildren—the children of the drug user. In some cases they are disconnected from the user. There are now a few services specifically for grandparents being established and your local drug support services should have information about relevant groups in your local area.

Often, their dilemmas are whether to officially report what they believe may be child neglect to the relevant authorities and what the ramifications of this action may have for the family. At FDS we always use a 'there is no right or wrong decision' approach and encourage those involved to look at all the options and the potential consequences of each one before choosing the option that they can best live with.

Grandparents of drug users sometimes have easier relationships with them than the parents do and, in some cases, can communicate better and be positive influences. These grandparents should be encouraged to play mentoring and other supportive roles. Although, because of their age and lack of knowledge about the reality of drugs in today's world, it is very important to ensure that they are given access to reliable information.

When it comes to deciding whether to raise the issue of a drug-using child with a grandparent who may not be aware of the problem, FDS always recommends open and honest communication. Perceived shame, stigma, generational, cultural differences, as well as a fear that your own skills as a parent will be questioned can make it difficult. Remember—most grandparents care for their grandchildren very deeply and they may surprise you with their wisdom and understanding.

When older relatives have their own mental and physical health problems, a parent of a drug user may decide it is best not to burden them further. Remember—whatever you decide is best for your situation is fine.

Our first major project was the establishment of our Telephone Support Line, manned 24 hours a day, seven days a week. Rather than operating as a counselling, information or advice service, its purpose is to lend support and be a listening ear. The first call came from Perth. I still don't know how they found out about us.

In 1999, FDS's Telephone Support Line statistics show a total of 5815 calls—an average of 112 per week, or 16 per day. By 2008 that annual figure had climbed to a whopping 28 263 calls—an average of 544 per week, or 77 per day. Word continues to spread and, sadly, the need continues to spread also.

My wife Sandra was enormously supportive from the start, and continues to be so today. When Damien first told me that he had been using drugs, Sandra and I had only been going out together for about nine months and were moving towards the idea of a committed relationship. It was a difficult beginning.

Having supported me through those early days of grief, Sandra also supported me in my vision to start FDS and was, from the very beginning, a committed volunteer. She attended the first training group we did for telephone volunteers and was determined to be actively involved—something that she has never shied away from since. Back then, we only had a very small number of members and volunteers, and the people who were involved were doing multiple shifts to try to cover all the hours in the day and ensure that nobody's phone call went unanswered. Sandra and I, in particular, were doing lots of shifts, and during that time it became very obvious to me that Sandra had people skills that I really don't have—endless patience and kindness and empathy. They were skills that were critical to the success of FDS. She enrolled in a drug and alcohol course and studied part-time, over two years, to gain more understanding of drug issues.

Sandra became the FDS telephone and volunteer manager and has remained an essential part of the FDS story and certainly an essential part of my life. We've been together now for over twelve years, got married in 2007, and even though she doesn't like the limelight and stays away from the public face of what FDS does, I am sure that most of the volunteers will tell you how important she is to FDS. Ironically, shortly afterwards someone close to Sandra became involved in drugs and we shared that journey together with a very positive outcome.

My daughter Gillian, now 39, was also very close to Damien. She personally helped him through detox and, like all of us, misses him terribly. I think his death helped turn her life around and she is now a primary school teacher.

My youngest son, James, 22, has Asperger's syndrome—a form of 'high functioning' autism. He was also very close to Damien but was unable to go to his funeral—something

I believe impacted on his ability to come to terms with the death of his much-loved older brother. At 16, he started using cannabis—the worst thing for someone with his condition. Today, thanks to his mother Christine, and his own determination, he has now stopped using cannabis and alcohol and is making good progress.

These days, FDS now has more than 200 volunteers and over 2000 members, with support groups—an alternative to the twelve-step groups like Nar-Anon and other more directive-oriented, tough-love groups—and courses running across Sydney, as well as other cities and regional centres. Our bulletin, *FDS Insight*, which started as a two-pager, is now a 48-page booklet which goes out bi-monthly to families across Australia and contains up-to-date articles, poems and stories from families who understand what it is to live with drug use.

A parent education kit, 'A Guide To Coping', contains information and strategies for families with drug problems and now appears, in part, in this book in Chapter 7.

People come away from our courses with an increased understanding of drug use and the knowledge that the way they react to the problem can guide them to a better solution. I discovered from our earliest group sessions that simple education on things like 'The Stages of Change' model (detailed here in Chapter 6), combined with a safe environment to 'tell their story' and receive support, enabled attitudes to change, and participants started to report positive outcomes and strengthened familial relationships. We teach people that, although they can't really do much about controlling their son or daughter's drug use, they can do something about controlling their own potentially negative behaviour.

Over time, I have seen fathers—men whose initial reaction to their child's activities was to order them out of home—gradually change their attitudes and become supportive of their loved one and guide them through lapses and other difficulties. I have also seen mothers—women who had previously reclaimed property from hock shops to 'keep the peace'—start to construct definite boundaries and engage their child into contracts with workable consequences.

One of the most difficult things for families to come to terms with is that their preferred goal of 'getting them off drugs' may not be achievable as quickly or as easily as they would like. Explaining to family members the reality of the 'long haul'—the fact that it may take many years to get through the drug-using process—without ever taking their hope away, is the most difficult task. Some families enjoy successful outcomes relatively quickly. Other families struggle for years through the ongoing cycle of hope and despair with little apparent progress.

FDS is a caring, non-religious and non-judgemental organisation—primarily made up of dedicated volunteers who have experienced first-hand the trauma and chaos of having family members with drug dependency. Having travelled the same road, our collective aim is to assist families across Australia to deal with drug issues in a way that strengthens— rather than disintegrates—families and achieves positive outcomes for all involved.

We have achieved our success with inadequate government funding and no support from corporate Australia. No company wants to be associated with drugs. Our volunteers and board have been the source of our strength, especially in the early years, and we owe a lot to a dedicated band of people.

At FDS we believe that families are important. They are the ones who, in most cases, understand their family member better than any professional. If left in isolation, though, families can become exhausted and give up. When properly supported, they can become a vital force for positive change.

Whether worrying about the needs of the entire community, or simply the individual needs of your drug-using family member, I realise that the problems associated with drug use can, at times, seem overwhelming. Yes, there is so much to do, but with help and guidance it really can be done—we just need to do it together. You are not alone.

CHAPTER 4

The Warning
Signs

When families find their way to Family Drug Support—either by telephone, or in person at one of our weekly support meetings—the same questions inevitably arise. One question that I am often asked is: 'How did I miss the warning signs?'

In fact, the feeling from so many parents is that perhaps they missed the indicators that could have helped them realise the presence of drug use in their child's life, 'before it was too late'.

First, I would like to say this: I don't believe that it is ever too late. I have seen too many families who come to FDS find hope where they once thought there was none.

Second, if you have missed the warning signs, it does not make you a bad parent.

I missed them too. In hindsight, they were definitely all there, but hindsight is, of all the forms of wisdom, the most unforgiving. I think everybody sees the signs when they look back, but, really, what is the point of looking back?

For those of you reading this book in the hope that it may help you to prevent a situation that has not even occurred yet, my advice is to please treat the topic of warning signs cautiously.

For parents, the question of 'Are they on drugs or just adolescents being adolescents?' presents a *damned if you do, damned if you don't* scenario. Being overly suspicious and wanting to always be in control of almost everything your child does is usually met with resistance, more secretive underground activity and also more of the negative activity you were trying to prevent in the first place. It can produce the very thing you are trying to avoid.

But if you try to do the right thing in allowing a transition time to occur, to properly monitor your child's behaviour over a period of time, you may, unwittingly, be allowing yet more dangerous drug use by not recognising the true situation and therefore not intervening in the earliest stages.

Linda, 57, first suspected that her daughter Rebecca, now 32, was using drugs at the age of 14.

I think the one main thing that I have learned from this whole episode is to trust your natural instinct. That little tiny voice that niggles at you all the time. That's what you should be listening to because that's what will often lead you on the right path.

All the advertising that you read and hear— about warning signs and whether there is huge

behaviour change and things like that—that's what
had happened and I just thought that it was drugs.
She'd gone from a very caring, loving young girl to
becoming this very secretive girl. I think if you asked
me what parents should be looking for, I would say
the secretiveness is a big thing.

With my youngest daughter, although she did
go through a bit of a character change when she
was going through that teenage stage, it wasn't as
aggressive or concentrated as the other one. Trust
your instincts.

It is very important to know that over 90 per cent of all
teenage drug experimenters DO NOT become long-term drug
users, and abandon any problematic drug use as they grow
into the responsibilities of adulthood. However, those of you
reading this book may not be in this category. Your family
member may be in a situation where the problems associated
with their drug use have already escalated to a dangerous
level, and are causing distress.

Sure, I can give you a list of things to look out for, or
point you to a number of websites—both Australian and
international—that detail a checklist of 'signs' that are
supposed to enable worried friends or family members to
leap to the conclusion that someone they know has a drug
problem, but even with such lists, I am sure that many people
will still find it hard to accept the reality.

Experts will tell you that typical signs of drug use are
someone who is irritable and cranky and sleeps a lot for
extended periods, or stays awake for other long periods and
then has sudden bursts of hunger, someone who doesn't eat

proper meals, someone who stays out all weekend and grunts at you instead of communicating with you, and someone who gets irrationally angry at you for no particular reason. Recognise any of those signs? Well, they could be signs of drug use, but they also, just as accurately, could be signs of a normal teenager dealing with the huge changes to their body and social lives and experimenting with those first stretches of soon-to-be independent, adult wings.

No matter how the evidence mounts, there is always that denial, of not wanting to accept what so many other people can see. Even when the signs are obvious, as parents or family members we do not want to admit that someone we love has a drug problem. The thought is too foreign and too painful and frightening. At FDS meetings, comments that 'he was such a good boy', or 'I never imagined she would get involved with something like this' are common.

Even more frequently, we hear 'he/she was okay until they formed a friendship with . . .'. It's easy to blame new friends but it doesn't change the reality—our son/daughter is now using drugs.

In most cases, teenagers will have been using drugs for weeks, months and sometimes even years before parents become aware.

Of course, in many cases, the existence of some warning signs has little to do with parental paranoia and definitely requires a stronger reaction. There are more obvious things, such as 'pinned eyes' (pupils that appear as tiny as pin pricks) that might indicate heroin use, while dilated pupils are a sign that they may be using stimulants such as speed and ecstasy. Track marks (the evidence of injection sites) on their arms is another big warning sign, as is sudden, massive weight loss, which could point to use of appetite-suppressing amphetamines. But it's still surprising that, even with these very clear indicators, some friends and family members still deny that there is any cause for concern. Because considering the alternative—the reality that someone you love is a drug user—is too worrying.

The parents who obsess over searching for these warning signs—the same parents who often riffle through their child's personal belongings, read private journals or emails, check mobile-phone texts and voice messages—are the ones who often make any potential rift between themselves and their child or other family member even harder to mend. Remember: modelling trustworthy behaviour means not taking on the part of private detective. Model trust and you are more likely to get it.

In an article entitled 'Surviving Terrible Teens', in Melbourne's Sunday *Herald Sun* newspaper on 30 September 2007, Dr Michael Carr-Gregg, a psychologist and author specialising in teenage behaviour, was quoted as saying that parents shouldn't be frightened of 'upsetting your teenager when it matters'. 'If you're the parent of an adolescent girl and you haven't had an altercation at least three times a week—you're not trying,' he said. He also went on to remind parents to put any fears and concerns into perspective to avoid unnecessary alienation. 'Parents need to make sure that what they're upset about relates to their child's safety and wellbeing. If it doesn't relate to that—it doesn't matter,' he said. 'Don't worry about untidy bedrooms. Don't worry if your teenager's hair is the colour of an exotic butterfly. Nobody has ever died of that.'

If your family member cannot trust you—if you have repeatedly come to them with accusations about their behaviour based on 'evidence' gathered by your invasion of their personal space without their permission—they will not come to you when there really is a problem. Your reaction, they know, will be one of outrage and anger, rather than one of patient, non-judgemental understanding.

Treat your family member with love, respect, and as much trust as you can muster, even when your natural instinct might be telling you to tighten their curfew or micro-manage their friendship groups and social life, and you may be rewarded by someone who feels that, when things are going terribly wrong in their life, they really can turn to you and be open and honest about what they are going through.

Wouldn't it be better to be the one your family member turns to in a crisis, rather than the one that they are afraid to confront?

With my son Damien, there were obvious signs but nothing that made me think that the problem was definitely drugs. I had wondered if he was in some sort of trouble, and had, admittedly, wondered if drugs *might* be involved, but even then I was probably only thinking about marijuana, and certainly never dreamed of heroin—I just never thought he would.

Ask most teenagers why they try drugs in the first place and the answers will most likely be more about 'fun', peer pressure, the need to feel part of a group, the desire to socialise with friends, boredom, the need for relaxation, or just simple curiosity, rather than a desperate need to combat depression or unhappiness. In other words, they take drugs for much the same reasons as adults—perceived positives. No one tries drugs to die or go to jail.

Amanda, 26, went from being a hard-working high-school student to injecting heroin.

I don't really think that there was any issue that led me to trying drugs. I was at school and was quite

experimental. In about year twelve a friend told me that I had to try this amazing drug, and I had smoked a bit of pot already and wasn't shy of giving things a go. She hung out with a bunch of older guys who were using heroin and we all did it this particular night. That was my first exposure to it. I closed my eyes, put my arm out and let this guy inject me with heroin. I might have tried speed once or twice but there was nothing really in between—just me being happy to try something new.

I remember being afraid of the needle but I still quite calmly stuck my arm out and let someone do that to me. I remember feeling like I was melting into the couch and this incredibly relaxing feeling came over me, but then I proceeded to vomit for most of the night. I don't know why that didn't turn me off completely but after that I used a few more times with this girl from school and her mates. Then I discovered Cabramatta. This was at a time when I was under a lot of pressure at school—doing really well and studying pretty damn hard but in between that driving out to Cabramatta with another friend who had also tried it with us. It was just too easy. You'd go past the chemist and pick up needles and then you'd go down the street and put your hand out and someone would tell you how much you had to pay and you'd hand it over and then take the drugs and that was that.

For parents or friends wishing to confront someone they believe may be using drugs, I firmly believe that knowledge is power. By arming yourself with up-to-date and honest facts about particular drugs, rather than bombarding the suspected user with an argument that is more about scare-mongering and tabloid-journalism-style paranoia, there is a better chance that some of your message might actually get across. Broach the subject calmly, in a quiet moment, rather than at the height of any other tension. Try to point out the health and lifestyle risks but don't push the point when you feel that their concentration is shifting. Sometimes you may have to accept that they will not immediately stop their drug use, regardless of what you say. At this stage, you want your position—that you love them but do not approve of their drug-taking and that you are worried about their welfare—to be made perfectly clear, without making them feel too pressured by your questioning and concerns. Using 'I' statements rather than 'you' statements makes for better communication.

For example, instead of using statements like:

You are ruining your life.
You have to stop this.
You will end up in gaol.

Use 'I' or 'we' in ways such as:

I am really concerned about…
I believe/think…
We don't like/would like…
We want you to know…

Monitor their ongoing behaviour carefully and unobtrusively and seek help for yourself, if needed. Help is out there and, even if it can't give you a magic fix that will immediately put an end to their drug use, it can help you learn strategies in order to cope with the path ahead. It sounds simplistic but, in many cases, the simple advice to 'trust your instincts' can work wonders. You know your child or family member well—perhaps better than anyone else and certainly better than any 'experts'. You don't really need to tick matches off a checklist to confirm that something is not right. What you do with that realisation, though, is what can make all the difference.

Where communication has totally broken down, I recommend writing a letter, an email, or a text—expressing your thoughts, feelings and beliefs: i.e. 'I believe that you are still using drugs and I know I can't stop you but I am always here to help if you need to talk.'

Chidem, now 27, was just 17 when her habit of smoking marijuana at weekends or at parties evolved into a heroin dependence. She avoided contact with her family for four years—believing that their pain would be lessened if they could not see what their daughter had become.

I don't know if there's anything parents can really do to stop their kids from trying drugs, but I do think that if parents try to get too strict—try to ban their kids from seeing certain people, or lock their kids up if they are suspicious—it can actually make it worse.

I think that if families can be open for the child to feel comfortable about what they are really doing and where they are really going, that can be the best thing. I do drug and alcohol awareness at high schools now through Family Drug Support and I realise that a lot of kids lie to their parents because they feel that they can't talk to them. Those lies could lead to kids doing things like I did.

I talk to kids about the reasons why people like to use drugs and then I talk to them about harm minimisation approaches around that. Kids take risks, so I try to ensure that, if they do take risks, they do it with their eyes open. And for parents—knowing that kids do take risks and there's not much you can do to stop that—try to make your child feel that they can come to you, no matter what.

CHAPTER 5

Building Bridges, Building Strength

By the time you have realised that there is a drug problem within your family, many other things might have already fallen away. Relationships might be in tatters—torn apart by secrecy, suspicion and anger—and, for many families, the repairs needed to rebuild these bridges can sometimes seem too huge to even contemplate.

If that rebuilding is done, though, strength as a family will also be rebuilt. It will take time—in some cases perhaps years—but I believe that, with patience and love, it can be done. And although you cannot do it alone, in order to begin this rebuilding, the groundwork does have to be just about you.

Remember, you cannot control anyone—particularly if their judgement is clouded by the effects of drugs. You can, however, work to control yourself and how you cope with the situation you have found yourself in—no matter how tough maintaining that self-control might seem.

If someone you care about has developed a serious dependency on a drug—any drug—it can obviously be very disruptive to your life, as well as to the lives of everyone who loves and cares about them. It is important, though, to try to identify the difference between the effects of their actions that cause actual harm to your life and the effects of their actions that simply leave your feelings hurt.

It might be incredibly hard to make this distinction but it is a very necessary one for a lot of people who are involved in the life of a drug user. Often, what is happening as a result of your loved one's drug or alcohol problem is that you are left feeling constantly hurt, disappointed, anxious and maybe angry as well. These feelings should not be dismissed and obviously have a huge bearing on your ability to cope. Hurt feelings are sometimes as harmful to your wellbeing as actual physical pain and, of course, your feelings are important and serve as a guide to your subsequent decisions. Too much harm and anger can definitely be harmful to your peace of mind and, perhaps, as the effects of stress take hold, even your physical health.

What I am suggesting, though, is that you pause for a moment to figure out the difference between your emotional reactions to your loved one's drug use (which may range from anger to disappointment to worry to hopelessness), and actual destruction. Are you losing money? Sleep? Your job? Are you and other family members feeling victimised or physically threatened?

At FDS, we believe that there are some behaviours that should NEVER be tolerated—especially violence and bullying. In some circumstances, it may be necessary to call the police and/or crisis teams. Other options may be to take out an Apprehended Violence Order (AVO), or have the drug user removed from your home. It is important, always, to let the drug user know the difference between loving them and not tolerating their behaviour.

Other negative behaviours, such as stealing, staying out until all hours, or using drugs at home are not always so easy to be black and white about. You should always look at all your options and the consequences of each choice—then make your decision. If in doubt, follow your own heart rather than the well-meaning advice of friends. If you feel that you have to ask your drug user to leave home, don't rush into it. A 'planned exit' is usually better than throwing them out into the street in the heat of an argument. Affirm your core values and needs, but beware of 'tough love' approaches.

I was the original 'tough lover'. I think most men are, as we are problem-solvers—we want to fix things, and this can often lead to threats, ultimatums and 'forcing' them into treatment. These are normal reactions for many men but they are a form of control and rarely work the way we want them to.

On the other hand, women often use their own methods of control—usually being overly sensitive and concerned. It is a woman's natural instinct to want to support everyone—the user, their partner and everyone else in the family system. At best, they are jugglers, trying to keep everyone functional, and at worst they become overly responsible rescuers with very poorly defined boundaries.

Those extreme examples of masculine and feminine 'control' also create winners and losers and can lead to relationship problems between parents—right at a time when the family unit needs to be stronger than ever.

Of course, not all men are 'black and white' thinkers and not all women are 'over-involved'. Sometimes, roles are reversed, and in a single-parent situation the control often switches between male and female reactions. Working together with a joint approach is usually the best way to get positive results. Black and white thinkers need to become more flexible in their responses and jugglers need to develop firmer boundaries and learn to look after themselves as well as others.

There is still so much ignorance and shame associated with drug use. It has diminished a bit but, sadly, maybe only a tiny bit. When a family member has a drug problem, there is already so much secrecy involved, but the most important step towards any possible recovery is to open your arms rather than turn your back, and to keep lines of communication open. I will say that a lot throughout this book, because it is true. Honest and open communication between yourself and the drug user is vital if there is to be any positive outcome in the future.

When confronted with the possibility that your family member might be using drugs, denial is something that is a universal experience (outlined in 'Stages of Change' in the next chapter), and, in essence, is something that is good for you in that it is a protective psychological safety mechanism that stops you falling beneath the weight of what you are going through. Without some form of denial, if you fully understood the ramifications of what was happening to your life, you might just collapse under the strain.

There is a time, though, when denial must stop, and you need to be strong enough not to collapse; a time when you must do all that you can to find the strength needed that is critical to ensuring your own survival and perhaps that of the drug user.

Why?

One of the principles that I firmly believe in is that families are very important, and that while professional counsellors and treatment specialists have their place, it is families who are often more skilful in dealing with their drug-using family member. However, in order to do so, they need a lot of awareness about the issues surrounding drug use—a world about which they probably have very limited knowledge— a few skills to help them become more effective in their approach to the drug user, and, of course, that much-needed emotional support that will help maintain their own sanity throughout such turmoil and uncertainty. At FDS we have living proof that hundreds of families who have applied these principles are coping better and are more resilient. Consequently their communication and relationship with the drug user is better and in many cases the drug user is much healthier.

Although it seems overwhelming, you really can help your drug-using family member. Realising that, and then working hard to gain the skills, support and awareness required, is an enormous step forward—not just for you but also for the drug user and anyone treating the drug user.

It is important never to give up hope—even though, of course, there will be many times when it truly feels that all hope is lost. Maintain your own strength in whichever way works for you and you will find that bridges really can be rebuilt.

CHAPTER 6

Stages of Change and Stepping Stones to Success

I developed what I call the *Stepping Stones* model as a way to help people who are affected by a family member's drug use to find a better, more supported way to deal with the processes that subsequently occur. To completely understand the philosophy behind it, and to gain the most benefit from the principles, people who feel that they do need extra help and support are recommended to enrol in the course through their nearest Family Drug Support office.

For those unable to do this, or for people who wish to glean a better concept of what the course will offer, the information in this chapter will still help enormously, because it will enable you to understand what both you and the drug user are going through—one of the very important first steps towards a potentially happier, healthier future. Read it and apply it to your own life, and I believe that some positive change will come. Change does not happen overnight but, with perseverance and patience, it can help guide your way through what can, at times, seem such a dark and lonely place.

Remember—you are not alone. However, by the time most people find us at Family Drug Support, loneliness is exactly what they feel. For many, the stigma and shame of having a drug user in the family has meant that even close friends and family—usually the sounding boards for all kinds of personal troubles and secrets—are not confided in. Even if they are told, their resulting reaction—often shock, followed by uncomfortable and unhelpful silence from people who just don't know how to support you—can only lead to you feeling further shame, isolation and secrecy.

You might feel that nobody will understand your pain or what you are going through, but, really, you are not alone.

When there is a drug user in the family there is a lot of confusion. The main question everyone asks is: 'How did this happen to me?' To answer that, we tend to turn those questions around: 'Why do you think it's happened?' By getting family members to talk about it and open up about what they think the reasons might be, they come up with their own answers. Knowing there is a 'road map' and that you are not alone is comforting and helps you feel normal. This is the first key point of Stepping Stones.

Drug use within a family is something that can happen to anyone. Dismissing drug problems as afflictions of the poor, poorly educated or dysfunctional is simply not true. I have seen people in the most exclusive suburbs battle with the same issues as people from stereotypical poorer areas. Drugs do not discriminate. It is common to feel shame or a sense of failure when you discover that someone you love is a drug user, however it is not your fault. It does not mean that you are a bad parent. Surrounding yourself with blame and shame will not allow you to move forward on your journey and should be dispensed with as soon as possible in order to really help yourself and the drug user.

Understanding the nature of drug use and typical feelings that both the drug user and the people close to the drug user experience is just one stepping stone on the path to recovery—but it is one that must be taken if you want the situation to improve.

In 1986, two US psychologists, Procheska and Di Climente, developed a model to define the various changes that clients will move through in order to change their behaviour. The first thing to get to grips with is that drug use is a process. There are stages for the user: Happy User, Ambivalence, Determination, Action and Maintenance (Procheska and Di Clement, *Stages of Change Model*). Progress is generally circular through the stages, although lapsing is a normal part of the process. People can 'lapse' and move between these stages at any time; although it may be helpful to know that when they do lapse they usually go back to ambivalence—not the 'happy user' stage.

Stages reflect the idea of moving forward through a process. Each individual's progress varies and is affected by their environment, circumstances and the type of substance being used. Moving forward may often take far longer than we might wish. People may go around this cycle a number of times and at any point might lapse to their old behaviour. It is not the end of the world—it is, in fact, normal.

While the drug user is going through these common stages, families, too, have a process that also involves stages of change: denial, emotion, control and chaos. These stages

Stages of change for drug use

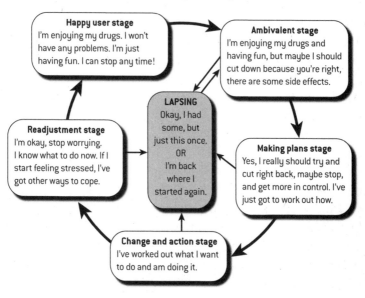

Happy user stage
I'm enjoying my drugs. I won't have any problems. I'm just having fun. I can stop any time!

Ambivalent stage
I'm enjoying my drugs and having fun, but maybe I should cut down because you're right, there are some side effects.

LAPSING
Okay, I had some, but just this once. OR I'm back where I started again.

Readjustment stage
I'm okay, stop worrying. I know what to do now. If I start feeling stressed, I've got other ways to cope.

Making plans stage
Yes, I really should try and cut right back, maybe stop, and get more in control. I've just got to work out how.

Change and action stage
I've worked out what I want to do and am doing it.

tend to repeat until exhaustion and disconnection occur, or until support, coping strategies and resilience can be found.

A typical first-time phone call to FDS might be: 'I'm throwing my son out on the weekend.' Instead of us saying that might be a good or bad idea, we would ask: 'Well, why have you come to that decision?' Then they may say: 'Well, he is stealing money and he lies and he's rude to his brother', and all the other negative things that have been going on in the house. So then we might say, 'Okay, so you're throwing him out but you're ringing us—why?' We just try to open up a conversation to try to figure out what's been happening.

Asking questions such as: 'What does your heart tell you?' or 'Are there any other alternatives that you haven't thought of?' can get family members out of their place of frustration and anger and often get them thinking of other possible options. Once they realise that it's not just a simple choice between putting up with the crap and kicking their child out, they start to get creative.

A woman rang Sandra once and said that she'd had enough and that she'd found a bag of marijuana hidden on top of the fan in her son's room, and was about to throw it away. Sandra asked her about all the possible ramifications of doing this—the fact that her son might be angry that she had been searching his room, his defensive reaction to knowing that his mother had discovered he was using drugs, and the fact that he might then respond by leaving the family home and missing his college exams—and then, at the end of the conversation, Sandra said, 'What are you going to do?' and the woman replied, 'I'm going to put the bag back on the fan.' This demonstrates that people will find their own answers without having to be 'told what to do'.

One father contacted me whose son had been deputy head boy at one of the major private schools, captain of the cricket team, leader of the orchestra, had achieved a TER score of 99.9 and was six months into medicine at Sydney University. Then he had dropped out, disappeared, and his family found him six months later, tattooed, pierced, living with a girl in Kings Cross and on heroin. This father came in to a support meeting and for the first three or four weeks all he could do at that meeting was vent his anger. When people vent their anger like that, you can't talk to them about process or control because they haven't even got there yet. You can't talk about what the future is possibly going to be because they just want to talk about where they are at right then. In terms of the stages that I believe people move through in these types of circumstances, this man was textbook, and he then moved straight from that anger into control mode. At one subsequent meeting he came armed with literature from the Internet about all these different programs and rehab alternatives and how he was just trying to fix it all. Then, finally, that control phase moved into acceptance and the realisation that he just had to hang in there with his son and it might, eventually, end.

Now his son knows that if he does need to go home, his father's not going to be in his face—pushing him to see this doctor or that counsellor, or coming down on him for his behaviour. If his son feels that home is a safe, non-judgemental place, it might be a place that he wants to go to when he's in trouble. That's an important message to get across. This particular father did eventually learn this, but it took a long time to get there.

After many unsuccessful attempts at detox, Amanda, 26, has now been drug-free for eight years.

The process that I went through to stop using was quite a long one. I kept falling back but my family were always there. Their support was ongoing. My father, especially, was blown away with everything that was going on and I think that having the information and knowledge that was given to them by FDS, plus the opportunity to talk to other parents who were in the same situation, made a huge amount of difference to them.

It's bloody hard. People who are abusing drugs push the boundaries beyond an acceptable point. It's incredibly difficult watching someone you love going through all this, but don't give up on them.

THE PROCESS

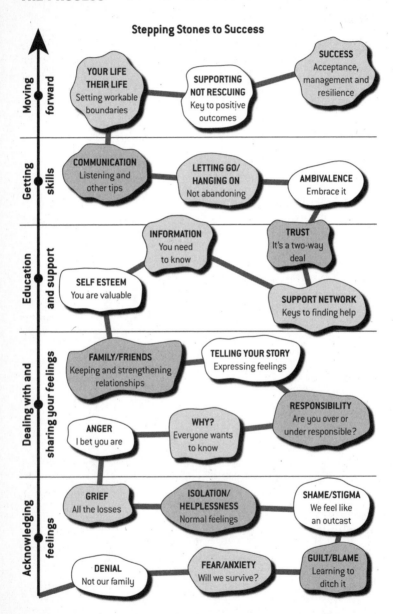

Stepping Stones to Success

Moving forward

YOUR LIFE THEIR LIFE
Setting workable boundaries

SUPPORTING NOT RESCUING
Key to positive outcomes

SUCCESS
Acceptance, management and resilience

Getting skills

COMMUNICATION
Listening and other tips

LETTING GO/ HANGING ON
Not abandoning

AMBIVALENCE
Embrace it

Education and support

INFORMATION
You need to know

TRUST
It's a two-way deal

SELF ESTEEM
You are valuable

SUPPORT NETWORK
Keys to finding help

Dealing with and sharing your feelings

FAMILY/FRIENDS
Keeping and strengthening relationships

TELLING YOUR STORY
Expressing feelings

RESPONSIBILITY
Are you over or under responsible?

ANGER
I bet you are

WHY?
Everyone wants to know

Acknowledging feelings

GRIEF
All the losses

ISOLATION/ HELPLESSNESS
Normal feelings

SHAME/STIGMA
We feel like an outcast

DENIAL
Not our family

FEAR/ANXIETY
Will we survive?

GUILT/BLAME
Learning to ditch it

Denial, Emotion, Control, Chaos, Coping

Stage One—Denial

This is where we really don't know what's going on in the life of the drug user, or we have put our head in the sand—even when we have seen signs. We hear what we want to hear because we don't want to acknowledge the truth.

We come out of denial in two possible ways—either gradually over time or, more commonly, because a traumatic event occurs. This could be an overdose, a large theft, a psychotic episode or some kind of legal intervention.

Stage Two—Emotion

Once woken from the denial stage, an intense emotional stage often follows. Feelings include guilt and self-blame—questioning what you might have done wrong to lead to this situation occurring within your family.

There is also fear—'what's going to happen to him/her?' —grief for lost hopes and dreams and then anger at the choices the drug user has made. With anger, we often rant and rave but this only results in causing more stress for us.

Stage Three—Control

The masculine solution is: when we have a problem, we fix it. It is often accompanied by a determined, zero-tolerance approach—part of the desire to get back to 'normal' as quickly as possible.

The feminine solution is often based around a desire to save everyone involved—the drug user, the husband/partner, the other children and other relatives. With this desire, women involved in the life of a drug-using child can often try to mask some of the actions of the drug user in the hope that it will cause less confrontation and help ease the tensions.

Single parents often vacillate between both types of control.

Any form of control—either masculine or feminine—never works.

Stage Four—Chaos

When control inevitably fails, we find ourselves in chaos. We feel incompetent and powerless. When a drug-using child is involved, parents can often pin blame on each other, causing their own relationship to crumble and meaning other siblings are under even more stress.

Stage Five—Coping

The good news is that there is another stage—coping. When families reach out to get help through support, education and awareness, they can learn skills in coping—including communication and boundary setting.

They can learn to 'have a life' and look after their own physical, emotional and spiritual wellbeing. The rest of the family are acknowledged and included.

While the drug user may still not be drug-free, it is a fact that, the healthier the family, the more likely the drug user will eventually respond positively.

TIPS IN THE EARLY STAGES

Seek help

When Damien was battling his own drug use, finding help was a very difficult thing. Not because I was bogged down by any male parental pride that made me want to keep my problems to myself—just because there was actually little help to be found. At least not the type of help I so urgently needed. Things have come some way since then, and although I believe that there is still a long way to go, help is out there.

At the back of this book there is a comprehensive listing of support services, and information about how to find out about treatment options all over Australia. For people in rural or regional centres, where services are limited or, sadly, non-existent, telephone support services can still be accessed, often toll-free.

Remember, though—you can't make your family member go to treatment if they do not want to go, and even if you do get them there, it may not be successful unless they really have the motivation and determination to help themselves. In these early stages, perhaps the greatest help you can seek is for yourself.

Learn about drugs

Arm yourself with knowledge. If you can, find out which drug they are using and how regularly. Learn all that you can about the drugs involved, the subsequent effects and the best treatment options currently available. Knowledge is power.

Stages of change for families

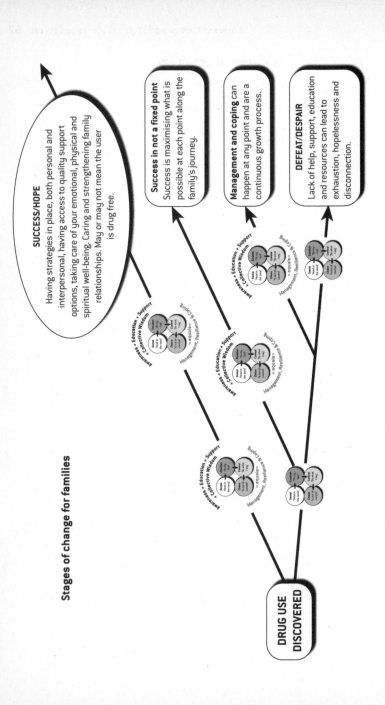

SUCCESS/HOPE

Having strategies in place, both personal and interpersonal, having access to quality support options, taking care of your emotional, physical and spiritual well-being. Caring and strengthening family relationships. May or may not mean the user is drug free.

Success in not a fixed point

Success is possible at any point along the family's journey.

Management and coping can happen at any point and are a continuous growth process.

DEFEAT/DESPAIR

Lack of help, support, education and resources can lead to exhaustion, hopelessness and disconnection.

DRUG USE DISCOVERED

Don't deal with things in isolation

Talk openly to your partner and the rest of your family and be sure to get support for yourself.

Listen to the drug user

Drug users tend not to want to talk much about their drug use, problems or feelings. Occasionally they will drop a hint or say they need to talk. Look for cues that they want to talk and then take the time to be with them and really listen, as calmly as you can. Having everything 'out in the open' is usually the best policy—despite the fact that it may be difficult. As a parent, it can be hard to hear your child talk to you about behaviour that you do not understand or sanction but, at this stage, if the lines of communication are opening up, the best way to keep them that way is to listen, rather than judge. Letting them know that you are worried about them is okay; telling them that you don't approve of what they're doing is also important; but reminding them that, despite your feelings about their drug use, you love them and will always be there for them is critical.

Try to avoid control and direction

Responding to their confessions with parental anger and control—such as forbidding them to spend time with a particular friend, imposing a curfew where there previously wasn't one, or searching their room and generally treating them with continual suspicion—will only lead to more secretive, underground activity and even more resistance to any positive change. Avoid using hidden agendas or strategies to get what you want.

When drug users are in the 'ambivalent' stage, for example, they are sorting out the pros and cons of using versus giving

AMBIVALENCE

'I want to use drugs but I don't want to'

Ambivalence is natural and normal — it is the heart of change

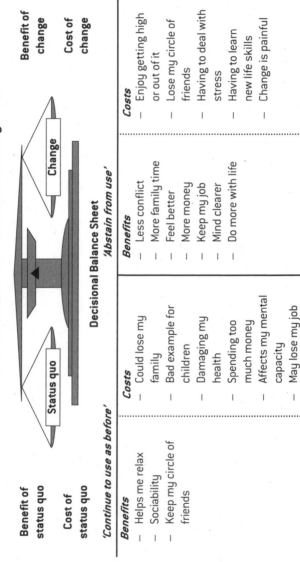

Decisional Balance Sheet

| | Benefit of status quo | Cost of status quo | Benefit of change | Cost of change |

'Continue to use as before'

Benefits
- Helps me relax
- Sociability
- Keep my circle of friends

Costs
- Could lose my family
- Bad example for children
- Damaging my health
- Spending too much money
- Affects my mental capacity
- May lose my job
- Wasting time/life

'Abstain from use'

Benefits
- Less conflict
- More family time
- Feel better
- More money
- Keep my job
- Mind clearer
- Do more with life

Costs
- Enjoy getting high or out of it
- Lose my circle of friends
- Having to deal with stress
- Having to learn new life skills
- Change is painful

up. Family members tend to push only one side of the balance scale—nagging to stop using and stressing the benefits of giving up drugs. This can actually be counter-productive. Try to be more empathetic and understand their dilemma—it will make it easier for them to make positive, informed decisions.

BASIC PRINCIPLES FOR SUPPORTING SOMEONE WHO USES DRUGS

- Open and honest communication is almost always the best policy. Listening is the most useful communication skill.
- Try not be judgemental, accusatory or emotional. Defer communication if you are not calm.
- Acceptance is not the same as approval. Just because you are not kicking them out of the family home, it does not mean that you are sanctioning their drug use, or giving them permission to use drugs under your roof. Telling them, in a calm way, that you do not approve of their drug use and behaviour, while, at the same time, reminding them that you love them and are there to help them, can reinforce your own views, without nagging them or alienating them further.
- When verbal communication is impossible or very difficult, try writing a letter.
- No one's drug use can be directly controlled by another person. You cannot monitor their every movement and so cannot ensure that they are drug-free—no matter how much you wish they were.
- Support is not the same as rescue. Let them know that you are there if they really need you, but don't come to their financial or emotional rescue every time they have a mini-

crisis. By keeping a reasonably close eye but still letting them make some mistakes, you are reminding them that you care, without being a doormat.

- Be clear on the boundaries. Take your cues from them. Their boundaries are usually very firm.
- Different situations demand different strategies. There is no 'right' or 'wrong' way of dealing with drug issues. It is no good doing something you are not comfortable with. Before taking action, think through the consequences and choose the one you can live with. 'Follow your heart' and be guided by your head and you will usually find the decision that is right for you.
- Separate negative behaviour from the person you love.
- Don't be afraid to talk to people and ask for help. Families also need help—not just the drug user.
- Be informed. Educate yourself about drugs and the issues.
- Understand the difference between dependence and casual or situational drug use.
- Be prepared for this process to take time, with only incremental steps forward.
- Remember—no treatment will work until he/she wants it to.
- Not every treatment is right for every person.
- Lapsing should not be seen as a failure. It is normal and is still a step forward.
- While you continue to love them you don't have to accept negative behaviour.
- Drug users have the right to be treated with dignity.
- Families have the right to peace and quiet.
- Most families have some influence over some aspects of the drug user, especially when the drug user lives at home or has regular contact. The drug user values food, shelter

and company but because many families don't realise this they don't 'bargain' with it.

- Expression of emotions and acknowledgement of feelings is therapeutic.
- Never give up hope.

For Liz, 60, by being open and honest about the family's problem, and learning more about what her son is going through, much of the stigma has gone.

Initially, there was shame around the whole issue of my son having an alcohol and drug problem, but over the years we've just become very open about it. The whole of the extended family have become aware of it and it's been a very healthy approach. There's no more keeping stuff secret—it's just all out in the open.

I have felt supported by friends and family and I think it would be incredibly difficult if it was different. Feeling alone would just add more stress to the stress that you are already going through.

I do think that the way I felt that I was being supported and helped did have an effect on the way my son has dealt with his drug problem. I have found that, the more knowledge I have—not only about the drugs but also about the cycles of change that both the users and the families go through—the more it helps everyone involved. It has given me the ability to have a really honest conversation with my son. We don't judge him—he knows that we love him dearly and we just accept that he has a drug problem. He does still have a drug problem but it has definitely decreased. The past eighteen months has been the best eighteen months we've had in a long time. He's not using as much, he's trying to get his life back in order, trying to get back into society and just having little lapses every now and then.

STRATEGIC HINTS FOR FAMILIES

- Be aware of hypocrisy—especially in your own use of substances. You may feel that your own use of alcohol or prescription drugs is a world away from your child's illicit drug use, but in their eyes it may mark you as hypocritical and damage any respect they have for you and the argument you are trying to present to them.
- Be aware of your own emotional state and the family dynamics in relation to the drug problem. All family members are affected and need acknowledgement and support. Every member can play their part in being able to invoke and influence change.
- Expression of emotion and acknowledgement of feelings is therapeutic. Sharing information with other families creates collective wisdom.
- Knowledge is power. Make sure that you accurately understand the nature and effects of different drugs. Seek information on all aspects of the drug issue, including treatment options, legal ramifications, overdose prevention, risks and responses. Know about tolerance and poly-drug use.
- Take things one step at a time. Encourage a harm-minimisation approach (see Chapter 9). Reduction, control and improvement of lifestyle can be an excellent start. Health and wellbeing are important. Using safely,

clean needles and vein care are examples of good harm minimisation.

- Abuse, particularly physical, should never be tolerated or accepted. If necessary, Apprehended Violence Order (AVO) procedures may need to be instigated. This does not have to mean abandonment but may have to be done—even if only in the short-term—to help yourself and other family members out of a potentially dangerous situation. Do not feel guilty about taking steps that ensure your own wellbeing or the wellbeing of others in the household.

- Avoid blaming yourself. At FDS we believe that families generally do the best they can with the knowledge, awareness and circumstances they have at the time. As you learn more, other options may become available. As I often say—knowledge is power.

- Don't rush into 'knee-jerk' responses. When thrown into a difficult situation—often without any warning—it is common for people to react without proper consideration. Try to pause, calm down, take a moment to think things through more clearly and you will increase your likelihood of making rational decisions.

- As a coping mechanism, it is tempting to break an established trust and search property, read private diaries and breach boundaries. Just remember, you have probably accused the user of lies, deception, manipulation and theft. To encourage two-way trust, you should ensure that you also deserve it in their eyes.

- Professionals have skills, knowledge, resources and expertise that can be extremely useful in helping families through difficult times, but families are usually the best people to judge when and which professional help is useful.

- In the case of siblings, even though it might be difficult, honest and open communication is the best approach.

Some siblings may be sympathetic to what is happening, others may be angry and antagonistic. It is important to acknowledge that you have heard and listened to their feelings, even if there is disagreement about family decisions that you make in particular situations. Even small children are better off knowing what is happening rather than being isolated from reality. Having acknowledged their feelings and opinions, it is important that the parents make the essential decisions jointly.

- Neighbours and friends often mean well and think they know what's best. They are not, however, directly living with the situation. If they offer advice it is probably best to listen politely, thank them and then make up your own mind. It is never any good doing what you don't feel comfortable with. There are no right or wrong answers but sometimes our 'gut feeling' tells us instinctually what we need to do. It is useful to safeguard yourself and the drug user from negative people, to prevent yourself and the drug user from receiving verbally or emotionally punishing behaviour.

- If your child has left home and is living on the streets, don't ask too many questions but be ready to listen. Try to contain your fear and control your anger. Offer food, coffee, a shower, or whatever may be necessary.

- If your child is in a refuge, contact the staff as a means of keeping in touch with their needs. Let them know if your door is open for them to come home, even if it's initially just for a good meal and a warm bedroom on a cold night. If they tell you about their experiences be prepared that some things may shock you. Sexual assault can occur, as can theft and prostitution for food and drugs. As hard as it is, try not to be too judgemental; remember, different rules apply on the street.

- Remind them of the importance of safe drug use and safe sex. If you find them with 'fit-pack' and needles and condoms be reassured that they are going to a Needle and Syringe Program. This means they are attempting to look after their own health. They are not sharing needles. They have access to health professionals for support, screening and sexual health advice. They are being supplied with clean injecting equipment, condoms, and when ready can be referred to treatment.
- Look after yourself. Take care of your physical, mental and spiritual wellbeing. For a positive outcome, you and the family have to survive the process too.
- Giving money when they ask for it is a vexed issue. You don't want to make matters worse and enable their drug use but you may fear they will turn towards crime or prostitution if you don't. Whatever you decide will be right for you, as long as you don't give more than you can afford. Don't get into debt to support their drug use. Above all, if you do choose to assist financially, don't harbour resentment about it.

GENERAL INFORMATION

- Know about the various services available to the drug user and to the family (see the end of this book).
- Know about dependence: physical, emotional and psychological. Be aware of the power of dependence (see Appendix).
- Know about the various detox options (see Appendix) and their impact on the user and family.
- Know about the pharmacotherapies: methadone, naltrexone and buprenorphine and others (see Appendix).

- Know about needle exchange programs. They are also valuable sources of information, support, advice and referral.
- Know about life after drug use and its impact on the user.
- Be informed about drugs and their effects and about available support services for the entire family.

COPING TIPS

- Understand the 'Stages of Change' model for the drug user (see Chapter 6). Accept lapsing as a challenge, not the end of the world. For example, if your loved one finally enters rehab after months of you asking them to but then only stays for one or two days, try to see the fact that they went as a positive step. Maybe next time they will stay longer.
- Understand the family 'Stages of Change' too. Look for workable options at whatever stage you believe you are in. In the emotional stage, find positive expression of your emotions. In the control stage, be aware of the potentially negative consequences of your actions. Always get support. Always utilise your 'balance pole'—all of the things that sustain you: friends, family, music, work, hobbies, sport, etc. Sustain and maintain your other relationships. Look after your emotional, physical and spiritual wellbeing.
- Don't put your life on hold. Continue to do the things you love.
- Walk away from confrontation. Many family members go through repeated, negative patterns of behaviour: i.e. every weekend they wait anxiously for the drug user to arrive home after a drug binge. A negative confrontation ensues and every week the parent feels dreadful. What could be done differently? One option is not to be around when the drug user arrives home.

By avoiding confrontation as soon as they walk in the door, any conversation can be had in a calmer way later. Of course, there may be sometimes occasions when there is a real threat to you or another member of the family. You may have experienced these violent situations before and dread them happening again. You fear the violent confrontation—yet you make no plans for if and when the situation occurs. It is a good idea to have a contingency plan in place. A sheet of paper with relevant emergency numbers—local hospital, local police, neighbours, trusted family members, etc. You may never need to use it but why not be prepared? Sometimes, in violent situations you may need to get away quickly. It is always better to leave—temporarily—than to risk physical harm to yourself or other family members.

- Set workable boundaries with acceptable consequences. Don't set yourself up for failure. Some ultimatums cannot be carried through. A common one is, 'If you don't give up drugs you will have to leave home'. A drug-dependent person is going to break this boundary—it is almost inevitable. So are you going to carry out the ultimatum and then live with the knowledge that they are on the streets because you told them to go? Probably not—and so you give them another chance and lose all your power. It is better to find a more realistic boundary that has more easily manageable consequences.

ACCEPTABLE GOALS

- Improved wellbeing of the drug user and of the family.
- Improved competence, confidence and management of drug usage within the family.
- Improved relationships within the family, with all people acknowledged and relationships strengthened.

- Improved emotional management.
- Improved problem-solving skills.
- Improved processes that effect positive change especially by solution-focused mechanisms.
- Believe in a win/win situation.
- A belief that you can 'have a life'—continuing to enjoy other aspects of your life, relationships, work and hobbies.

Dealing with drugs in the family changes things. We have to let go of some of our expectations and attitudes and we are often confronted with decisions we never thought we would have to face. We want our loved one to be drug-free. We want to be back to normal. No matter what we want, we sometimes have to come to terms with a different reality. It can be an incredibly hard road but you can survive.

Never give up hope!

Pam, 59, says that attending Family Drug Support meetings with her husband Bob, and undertaking the Stepping Stones program helped her find the resilience she needed to support her son through years of drug use. He is now drug-free and Bob and Pam facilitate regular FDS meetings to help others cope with similar experiences.

As a parent using FDS, I found that going to the meetings was really good reinforcement so it's a way of giving back to the organisation that helped us so much. It can be tough. As with so many things about parenting, the theory is really easy but it's the practice that was really hard.

When you are dealing with a person in dependence you just don't see any hope and you can't see if you'll ever get out of it. It's like a tunnel and you feel trapped by it. It's just chaotic and things are whizzing around everywhere. Nothing's got any order.

It's nice to be able to tell people that our son has been four and half years drug-free and to say: 'We went through exactly what you are going through now.' We don't tell our story all the time but it does help some people when they get really low. There are so many positive outcomes.

What do people get out of it? Coping skills. Coping with what's going on and coping with changes. What we're saying to them is, 'Although we do talk about the person in dependence a lot, we're really here about you. We're here about trying to give you the coping skills to make your life better, because whatever you do will make no difference to the drug user unless you keep yourself healthy and get out of their face, off their back and give them an opportunity to recover.'

I have already mentioned that the drug user goes through different stages of change with their drug use. Throughout these different stages there are different responses that may or may not be helpful. Here are some practical tips.

HAPPY USER STAGE

While the drug user is in what we call their 'happy user' stage, which is where they don't really have any problems and they think everything is good about drug use, families are typically in the denial stage, and, in combination, obviously there's not much happening. The drug user is keeping everything secret and believes that everything is fine, and the family are not really aware of what's going on. That stage often ends with a shocking jolt. It might be the police knocking on the door; overdose; finding a syringe or other drug-related implements; finding actual drugs hidden away; or noticing that money is going missing. Other people might find that their journey through denial is a long, drawn-out process and that it takes some time for reality to hit.

Tips to help them:
- be patient
- tell them you are there for them if they need it
- be open and honest in your communication with them
- listen.

Tips to help you:
- obtain information
- get support for yourself
- look for cues—when they want to talk, take time to listen
- encourage them to be honest about their drug use.

AMBIVALENT STAGE

In this stage, the drug user is often starting to weigh up the good and bad things about their behaviour. They have usually begun to realise that they may not be in control any more.

Tips to help them:
- be interested in them and their drug use—listen to what

they believe to be the perceived benefits of drug use, as well as their problems

- provide information to reinforce the good and bad aspects
- be willing to listen and continue to be patient
- remind them of their qualities and their talents.

Tips to help you:

- talk things over with others
- don't put your own life on hold
- try to understand the process (i.e. which stage they are in)
- communicate what you will and won't accept, in a positive way
- keep listening and don't push the 'give up' message too hard.

MAKING PLANS STAGE

In this stage people will be planning how they can reach their goals, deciding what they need to do, or who can help them.

Tips to help them:

- keep LISTENING
- help them get that information
- stay in touch—particularly if they are not living at home
- reinforce their plan
- be positive.

Tips to help you:

- develop workable agreements and the things you will accept, such as the behaviour you will accept when they are in your home
- look after yourself—physically, emotionally and spiritually

- don't always rescue them out of difficult situations (learn to let go)
- keep listening.

DETERMINATION STAGE

In this stage people are starting to take steps to make a difference in their lives. In drug-affected people this may be small, e.g. reducing their drug use, going into detoxification, avoiding friends who deal, not stealing, and seeking medical treatment.

Tips to help them:
- be positive about each step they take
- continue to be patient and listen
- acknowledge and celebrate their successes—no matter how small
- be realistic about lapsing and the difficulties associated with treatment.

Tips to help you:
- be available
- if asked, help them to get re-established, e.g. pay the bond for the electricity
- provide food and other practical help.

ACTION AND MAINTENANCE STAGE

In this stage people are practising their new behaviour and trying to make this part of their everyday lifestyle.

Tips to help them:
- don't test them by leaving money lying around to see if they take it
- model trust and other positive behaviour, such as resilience

and coping skills

- encourage them and quietly let them know how far they have come
- continue to listen and provide practical support.

Tips to help you:

- maintain support for their chosen goal
- don't expect too much too soon
- be available.

Remember, the new 'straight' person is readjusting to a whole new life and that can be really, really scary. Being straight after a long period of drug and alcohol use may be difficult for many people to cope with at first, and this can bring its own challenges.

Sometimes people want too much too quickly, i.e. having given up drugs they want other aspects of normality, such as career or educational prospects, or relationships, to resume instantly. It is important to encourage patience and remember that some things take time. Many people who do go onto methadone or other pharmacotherapies find aspects of their life become stable. The temptation then becomes to get off methadone too quickly—and this can lead to going back onto heroin. Substitute treatments work best when they are seen as long-term treatments.

A volunteer of ours, Alan, had a son who was on heroin. Crime was part of his life in order to support his use. Alan was a 'tough' dad and even dobbed his son in to the police in order to try to force change. Of course, this control didn't work, and eventually Alan got support for himself and started to change his attitude—eventually becoming a telephone volunteer on the FDS phone line. Meanwhile, his son, despite many setbacks, recovered. He did a medium-term rehab and then moved into a halfway house. Out of the blue, Alan rang me. His son had left the halfway house. When I asked Alan what he would do when his son eventually rang him, Alan, who had predicted that his son would have left the house to go on a drug binge, told me that he would ask his son to meet him for a coffee, that he would point out his progress and what he had achieved so far, and that he would also remind his son that this was just a hiccup. Things went pretty well, as Alan predicted, and now, several years later, his son is drug-free, married, with a child and his own business, and Alan himself is in a calm state of happy retirement. It can happen.

LAPSING

In this situation the person has again used drugs or alcohol. This may be a 'one-off' thing, or could be the first step towards them reverting back to chronic use.

Tips to help them:
- try to encourage them to feel they can try again when they feel ready
- be positive about what they have achieved so far
- suggest that next time they may be able to do more and get that little bit further along.

Tips to help you:
- try to understand that this process is normal
- remember their previous successes and try to keep calm
- encourage them and re-explain what has happened so they can see it as a 'slip-up' that they can overcome, rather than as a sign that they will never succeed
- continue to listen.

Remember, stages reflect the idea of moving forward through a process. Each individual's progress varies and is affected by their environment, circumstances and the type of substance being used. Moving forward may often take far longer then we might wish. *People may go around this cycle a number of times and, at any point, might lapse to their old behaviour.* It is not the end of the world—it is, in fact, normal. Expect that lapsing will occur and it will be easier to cope with the disappointment and get back on track.

After reuniting with her parents, Chidem eventually became drug-free and now works with Family Drug Support—educating teenagers about the risks involved in drug-taking.

One of the things that made me crumble sometimes was that, throughout all my attempts through rehab and detoxing, if I did something wrong and relapsed, I got stuck in thinking 'this is what I am—I can never make it, and this is what I am so I just have to accept it'.

I remember someone telling me 'once a junkie, always a junkie' and that really made me think—that's it and maybe I should learn to live with it and I'll just die one day. There are a lot of negative words out there but you just have to not listen to them. There is a lot of help out there to try, but remember that what might work for one person might not work for another. I have tried home detox, rapid detox in hospital, I've done rehabs and many different things. Keep trying and remember—if you do fall backwards,

just try again. It's a learning curve and you should
just try to remember the positive things that you have
learned along the way.

Depending on the substance involved and the length of their dependence, the drug user may have gone through incredible changes that are not easily overcome. Giving up a drug is one thing, but returning to a 'normal' life—perhaps after any concept of a daily work routine has long gone, and friendship groups have only included other drug users—is yet another challenge. The person may now have a criminal record—another hurdle that can be very difficult to overcome.

Once you have identified the stage that the drug user is at, an appropriate approach is easier to develop. Remember that your goals may be different. Your preferred goal may be that the person remains abstinent from all drugs. Their goal may be to reduce or control their drug use, or even to be abstinent from some substances but continue to use others—e.g. give up heroin, but keep smoking cannabis now and again.

Consider ACCEPTING the possible rather than demanding the ideal.

When you've got this kind of crisis in your life, it feels as though you are being pushed out onto a tightrope. Your first instinct, understandably, is to get back to the place in your life where you felt safe. At first, you try as hard as you can to get back there, but then you realise that you can't and that you really do have to get out there on the tightrope. That's when you need to start looking for safety nets.

There are a number of ways that you can find safety

The tightrope walk

The Balance Pole

This is a vital tool for any tightrope walker. It provides support and confidence. The pole is made up of all of the things that we need, right now, more than ever before. It shows that we, as individuals, are important, valuable, and that we will survive.

Sadly, the balance pole is the first thing we throw away as we try and do the journey alone.

- Education
- Family
- Friends
- Interests and passions
- Hobbies
- Faith/religion
- Sport
- Leisure
- Relationships
- Work
- Holidays
- Books
- Support groups
- And more ...

Life before the discovery of drug use is a safe and familiar place

Safety nets

- Issue unwelcome ultimatums
- Throw them out to force change
- Try magic bullets/cures

So tantalising and promise so much. We want quick fixes and for things to return to the way they were. Is this real? Do they work? Jumping into these supposed 'safety nets' only to find ourselves back at the start of the tightrope walk.

Letting go

Life becomes easier as we communicate openly and honestly. We have finally let go of our agendas and expectations.

Each person will get here at their own time through hard work.

When we get here, the relief is incredible!

Success

For some it may mean being free of drugs. For others it may be less harm, a reduction in use or some maintenance programme. By doing the hard work and nurturing all aspects of our balance pole, we begin to rebuild our foundation.

Despite the chaotic journey, family and other relationships become stronger.

nets. The main thing to realise is that you should have a balance pole to help you manoeuvre your own journey on the tightrope. At Family Drug Support, an important part of what our Stepping Stones program does is to encourage people to build up a really strong balance pole, because that's what will always help you move forward.

Your balance pole is everything that you've got—your friends, your family, your favourite music, your hobbies, your relationships, or your faith. I don't care where that support comes from in your life, as long as there is some support for you.

Although walking that tightrope might seem frightening, one thing to know is that, about two-thirds of the way across, there's a place called 'letting go', where everything becomes easier. It doesn't mean your problem is instantly solved and that your child is suddenly drug-free, but it does mean a substantial change has taken place to bring you to a point of understanding, compassion and acceptance.

When you let go, there's no longer any need to be pushy or controlling. It is extremely hard to parent a drug user—or be in any close relationship with someone who is using drugs—but in my experience, no matter how improbable it seems in the beginning, and no matter how precarious the tightrope walk gets, people who work hard to create change will always get to that point of being able to let go.

There will, no doubt, be times when you feel that you haven't moved on at all, but that feeling is often clouded by concern and frustration. If you take some time to properly reflect on where you've come from, you will realise that, really, you have probably done an enormous amount of great work.

With the ongoing help of Family Drug Support, Linda, 57, has supported her daughter Rebecca through the rehab process and now believes that her daughter is drug-free.

Stepping Stones gave me access to people that I could talk to who understood where I was coming from. To have your feelings validated is really important because when all this is going on you do start to feel that you might be going a little bit insane so you start second-guessing yourself. Family Drug Support and the Stepping Stones program enabled me to identify where I was in my journey and it gave me the tools to cope with what I was going through.

The majority of people who come to FDS meetings want to help support their kids—not turn their backs on them—so they need to learn the skills to do it, without enabling them. If I can help anyone get through it, with the experiences I have had, that makes me feel really good.

We still get the ongoing after-effect of all this in our lives, though, so I think I still need the ongoing support for myself too.

I don't think my daughter and I will ever really experience that normal mother/daughter closeness, but things have come a long way. My advice would be to never, ever take your love away from your children, keep that communication open and try as hard as you can to cop it sweet. It's not them—it's the drug. I look at Rebecca and I still see that child I gave birth to—not the drug addict. I think that's what you need to do— keep seeing them as that child you gave birth to and not the person who is being controlled by the drug.

During my time with Family Drug Support, I have heard some incredible stories and met many remarkable people.

A lot of people who have gone through the drama of this happening within their family say that they have become better parents and better people because they have had to deal with the problem. Obviously, they would much rather have never had to experience the pain and worry of it in the first place, but when they do come out the other side, they often do so as more tolerant, compassionate people.

As you are going through it, of course, the notion of you emerging as a better person is the furthest thing from your mind. Your main focus is to do whatever it takes to ensure the drug user's safety—a wish that has you longing for a drug-free existence. Just remember, though, that there are some things you cannot change—no matter how hard you try. You can, however, always work on changing your reactions to them.

GOLDEN RULES

Drug use is a part of modern-day human life and, whether we like it or not, it is unlikely that the world will become drug-free.

There are no formulas for success. Every person's journey is different and everybody will make different choices. Accepting that you are going through a process, just like the drug user, will make it easier to understand the various changes that occur.

If you care about your family, trust yourself to realise that you always do the right thing, even if your strategies may change from time to time.

Follow your own heart—often looking at all your options and deciding what you can best live with is a better path to take than the one that some other well-meaning people may tell you is 'the best thing to do'.

Use a constant process of 'Action Learning'—planning, doing, reflecting and modifying.

Look after yourself. Your emotional balance pole that contains all your resources—friends, work, hobbies, faith, family, sense of humour, and support networks—is what will keep you sane and give you the strength to go on.

TIPS FOR OVERCOMING STIGMA

- Communicate as openly and honestly as possible within the family.
- Seek help and support. It is not a weakness to ask for help, just as it is no feat of emotional and spiritual wellbeing.
- When you form opinions about the issue that has impacted so deeply on your own family, think about getting involved in a broader sense—lobbying for change on both a political and community level.
- Talk to other people about drug issues, including your family. Wherever possible, take the opportunity to increase awareness and educate others in the community.
- Challenge prejudice where and when you encounter it! Don't let ignorant people hold the floor.
- Celebrate your, your family's, and the drug user's qualities, talents and victories.

CHAPTER 7

A Guide to Coping

When drugs left their scar on my own family, I wanted information and knowledge in order to understand what my son Damien was feeling. I also needed to understand the raging nature of my own emotions, to have my own fears and concerns listened to and to have my instinctive responses to what was happening around me validated and treated with compassion.

When the war on drugs suddenly becomes part of your own family's story, even your own child can feel like an enemy. Anxiety can become your constant companion and you may find yourself asking the same questions, over and over. Will they:

- be all right?
- get sick?
- die?
- deal, steal and prostitute themselves?
- end up in jail?
- ever be the same again?

You also want to know: will your family survive?

Severe physical, psychological and behavioural symptoms arising from anxiety can start to affect all your relationships. Worry can give way to chronic stress. In most families, shame and embarrassment are factors that create a normal tendency to 'keep it within the family', and even grandparents, siblings and close friends may be kept in the dark because of this.

You can learn to deal with these often complex situations by gathering reliable information to answer your questions, and by learning coping skills to use within a framework for change and reduction of harm. You need not be alone. There is hope and support available, and FDS, through its services, has already seen many positive outcomes for families.

Unfortunately, there are still so many myths and misconceptions about drugs and drug users and this continues to perpetuate the shame and stigma experienced by families. The impact of this is that many families will continue to struggle on in secret, too ashamed and afraid to ask for help. A lack of awareness that a drug problem is actually a health issue, rather than an issue of eroded morality or a result of weakness of character, just adds to the silent turmoil that families dealing with these issues experience. Remember:

- Families usually do the best they can with the circumstances, information and support available to their particular situation.

- Families have the capacity to influence their drug user either positively or negatively. Influence is strengthened when the drug user is given family support.
- Just because you don't have the knowledge yet, it doesn't mean that you can't attain it. Family members can grow and adapt and build their skills, knowledge and expertise to deal with drug issues in their own family.
- Drug users and family members have the right to be treated with respect and dignity. Just because you have a drug user within your family, it does not make you a bad person.
- Family members have the right to peace and privacy.
- Working with the support of other families through collaboration is better than working alone.
- Change is inevitable but sometimes seems difficult to achieve. Changing your thinking from a focus on 'problems' to a focus on 'solutions' helps you create the family energy needed for change.
- Expressing emotions and acknowledging feelings is therapeutic.
- New wisdom develops as issues are dealt with and managed.
- Open and direct family communication is usually the most constructive approach.
- Success is determined by the belief that you have done all that was reasonably possible to improve the situation. Acknowledgement of achievements (even if things seem to be going badly) is important as part of the process.
- Maps and tools and diagrams can guide you to where you are, show where you are going and help you regain your way when you feel lost. They help you recognise that others too have travelled the same road.

Fay, 62, has supported her 33-year-old son through a 13-year heroin problem and now works part-time for FDS as their Community Development Manager.

At the meeting, as the facilitator, you don't give advice but instead you lead people around the table into making their own strategies. I think people appreciate the fact that I am not just reading out of the textbook. That's how FDS helps. A lot of the people leading the meetings know exactly what you are going through.

Many people do come in saying 'How do I fix this?' and they want a solution straightaway, but there is no easy fix and you have to tell them that. There is no right and there is no wrong. I would say: 'Why don't you talk about it and we'll see what steps you can put in place for yourself?' The solution really lies in the person who is taking the drugs, but in coming to FDS we can give you the tools you need to at least make your own life better.

Real change requires energetic and disciplined commitment, preferably with involvement of all family members. Every family member and their relationship within the family is important. It is also important not to push the rest of the family into the background. A resentful partner or jealous siblings will only lead to further complications and even greater stress. Each family member may require support at any time and all family members can play a part in change. However, even if the support of all family members is not available, effective change can be, and often is, still achieved with just one or two supportive and committed members of the family.

To help yourself cope through stressful times, it is important to ensure that the issues surrounding the drug user do not stop you from finding pleasure in what were once the daily habits of your life. If you were involved in a sporting club or regular social activity that you have felt unable to be part of, make the effort to resume it. Staying in touch with friends is important.

It may seem like strange advice—encouraging you to be involved in what may appear to be frivolous activities when things in your family seem so chaotic and on the verge of crisis, but it is important that you work to maintain some happy aspect of the 'old' you, to help minimise feelings of resentment and frustration with the drug user and the impact they have had. Outside interests and 'time out' for yourself will enable you to recharge your batteries and be better able to cope. By getting on with your own life and not being over-protective you are helping the drug user to face up to the problems that result from their choice to take drugs. You are also helping them to take more responsibility for the way they feel and act.

If the drug-affected person is a parent and the wellbeing of their child/children is a concern, you may, though, need to juggle your work and lifestyle to ensure their safety, and shouldn't be made to feel guilty if this is the case. A young child's immediate care, development and physical and emotional wellbeing often cannot wait for the period it may take the drug user to succeed. This may mean that you need to give more care, provide more respite and substitute parenting than you probably would have expected, had the circumstances been different.

Even if you yourself have shunned any outside help or counselling, that thinking may need to change if there are small children involved. Their needs are important and if, as children of a drug user, their lives have been chaotic and traumatic, a combination of abundant love, support and ongoing counselling may be needed to ensure that their own journey into adulthood does not mirror that of their parent/parents.

When faced with a situation that is unknown, fear is a natural response. It is natural for your mind to race ahead to envisage the worst possible outcome, but, in the majority of cases when drug experimentation is discovered, this is not the reality. Each and every step you take towards raising your own awareness about the issues surrounding drug use is a step closer to a positive outcome.

In learning better ways to cope, understanding the nature of drug use and the terms associated with drug use can be of some help. Without knowledge, the world of drug use is one that seems even more foreign and confusing.

DEPENDENCE

Dependence is a commonly used term in the world of drug users, but what does it really mean?

Dependence can be thought of in relation to physical aspects, psychological aspects and emotional aspects:

Physical dependence

Physical dependence means that not taking the drug causes unpleasant physical effects (e.g. being sick) that are relieved by taking the drug again. Physical dependence is followed by the development of tolerance. Tolerance is where the drug user needs to take more of the drug or drink more alcohol to get the same effect. Tolerance can develop fairly quickly depending on the amount, regularity and type of drug taken.

Psychological dependence

Psychological dependence means that the person is mentally focused on the drug's effects, constantly thinking about the drug and the feelings associated with taking the drug. This is also called 'craving'. Cravings come in cycles and it is possible to learn behaviours that can help the drug user ride the wave of cravings without succumbing.

Emotional dependence

Emotional dependence means the person uses the drug to avoid negative feelings or to just feel 'normal'. Despite much research, no one is sure why a small proportion of users of any drug will become dependent. Not all problematic drug use involves dependence but it can still lead to short-term problems. This might include intoxication, accidents, family conflict, violence or abuse, mental-health breakdown, dehydration, poisoning and overdose..

One thing is certain:

DRUG DEPENDENCE IS NOT INEVITABLE

Just as alcohol use among your friends may range from the odd drink to problem drinking to alcohol dependence, so it is with illicit (illegal) and licit (legal) drug use.

Remember, if you suspect that someone in your family is using drugs, maintaining as much love and trust as you can manage, while still arming yourself with as much knowledge as you can absorb along the way, is the best starting point.

TOLERANCE, DEPENDENCE AND WITHDRAWAL

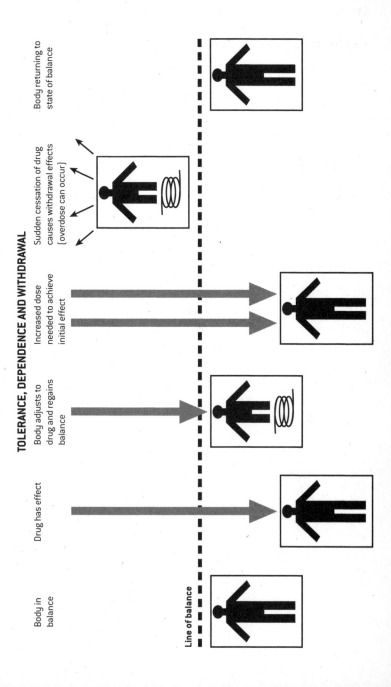

Body in balance

Drug has effect

Body adjusts to drug and regains balance

Increased dose needed to achieve initial effect

Sudden cessation of drug causes withdrawal effects (overdose can occur)

Body returning to state of balance

Line of balance

CHAPTER 8

You Can Do It

In my years with Family Drug Support I have spoken to thousands of families affected by drugs in one way or another. I have heard remarkable stories of courage, hope, perseverance, resilience, despair, grief and of course love. I cannot emphasise enough the power of storytelling and the impact personal stories have both on the listener and the teller. Many of our members have courageously told their stories publicly in forums etc. Here are a few more which tell of the struggles and triumphs of ordinary people dealing with huge impacts.

Bob and his wife Pam, both 59, have seen their son struggle through many dreadful years of drug abuse and believe that Family Drug Support gave them the strength to cope. Their story highlights the different approaches often taken by men and women in the lives of a drug user. As a father, Bob's first instinct was to try to fix the problem, while Pam's, as a mother, was to support and maintain her son. Through attending FDS group meetings, Bob learned to become more flexible, while Pam was taught how to develop boundaries—knowledge that enabled them to work together. Their son is now drug-free.

Bob: Our son Matt is now 32 years old and has spent roughly 10–12 years living with addiction. I suppose we went through all the usual stages of denial and trying to cope with it. He initially had a gambling problem. He was playing basketball with the local church team and they were dropping in to the pub after the game and he was playing those machines where it's like playing cards but electronic. He was 16, going on 17, and stealing a lot of money from our business. At that stage, he had already started to use drugs too—smoking cannabis—but we hadn't been aware. We thought it was gambling and that was it.

Pam: In his last year or so of school he started to get really angry about a lot of things. He moved out of home as soon as he finished his schooling and went and did a sound-engineering diploma course which really went nowhere. Then he did a hospitality course which led him to some work—it was shift work, odd hours. It wasn't really a great thing for him, living that lifestyle.

He was living out of home and never really had any money. We kind of just thought it was the gambling but by then I think he was pretty well into cannabis and I don't know what else. I think he was pretty much trying everything at that stage. I remember at his twenty-first birthday, his friends had, for a present, bought him a hit of speed. That was a rude awakening— thinking: 'this is what these kids do.'

Bob: His dependency wasn't intense all of the time—I mean, he started an apprenticeship as a cabinet-maker. He was about 22. It was something that he had always wanted to do and we hoped that it might settle him down, which it did for quite a while. He went through TAFE and he scraped through his exams but he didn't finish his last year. The drug use was just too bad.

Pam: At one stage he was living on the streets. He just didn't show up to work in the end. They had tried to look after him but he had abused their trust a bit. When he left, that

was when he fell over the edge. We
never told him to move out of home
but he was just living a very transient
lifestyle and never had enough money to
do anything.

He started doing rehabs within that time
too. We talked to him about doing some
treatment and he went into about 8–10
rehabs over the time, but sometimes he'd
just go in and not last.

Before he left home each time I always
had a piece of paper written out with all the
refuges on it. I just had to trust the system
because you can't hold them—they'll just go
when they want to. They're a free spirit and
the dependency makes them irrational.

I remember Bob ringing Family Drug
Support. I had been to a couple of the
Gam–Anon meetings but I found them just
like a knitting group. People didn't really
seem to talk about any solutions. They just
talked about their problems.

Bob: Tony seemed to have a different approach
to it, although when we first started I must
admit that I was very angry that I was going
to these meetings and yet Matt was doing
whatever he wanted to do and he was the
one with the problem. Certainly, I initially
went to find answers to cure him—not to
change us. It took me a while.

Then I started to learn things about handling Matt. Just that acceptance that you can control some things but you can't control everything. I was an air-traffic controller so I was used to telling people what to do and they did it instantly. I was a controlling person, so I suppose what Family Drug Support taught me was that there were ways to achieve objectives without being in control all the time.

Pam: I think a big thing with parenting is to come to terms with the track that your child has taken. It takes a lot, as a parent, to come to terms with your dashed expectations and to learn that you can't always control them. Learning that took the pressure off.

The change with us didn't happen overnight—it was over a period of four or five years. Matt was watching us change and then, really, in the end, he said that he wasn't going to go to any more rehabs and that he was sick of the lifestyle and that he was just going to give it up and that he had to do it himself.

He was also in a relationship with a young lady he'd met in rehab. That was pivotal. They used together for quite a while but then they both decided to try giving up together. They went cold turkey and both went to the Narcotics Anonymous program.

Matt rang and asked if they could both come and live with us while they tried to get clean. That was a very challenging time for us. They started doing some courses—they thought that if they tried doing a course in drug and alcohol it would be a really good idea, but it was just too much pressure. One day they showed a video of someone shooting up and his girlfriend just needed to feel the needle so that night they went out and used.

They were in a downward spiral after that—for about three weeks—and then Matt got toxic shock and ended up in St Vincent's. That was the closest he came to dying. He's never drunk alcohol or used since that day. He's working again now too—he now works in welfare in a group home.

There's no point in looking for any reason about why it's happened. It's happened and you've got to learn to cope with it.

Our relationship with our son now is wonderful. We always talked about it with our relatives and our friends and I think that was really helpful for us. They knew he was a really nice kid and, even when he did really terrible things, they were supportive and could understand that the behaviour wasn't him and that the drugs were causing this.

He was always still our son and we both always loved him.

Fay, 62, first sought help for herself in the earliest days of Family Drug Support's existence.

My son was about nineteen when he got involved in drugs. There wasn't much around for families then—nothing, really. I saw an advertisement for that first meeting Tony held at Ashfield, went with a friend and thought, 'these are the people I need to be talking to.'

I got involved in a 'help myself' way at first, then became a volunteer and then eventually started working for them. I guess I was just looking for somewhere that I could get some support from, and where you weren't made to feel like your child was a leper and the worst person on God's Earth. I had tried Lifeline and it just wasn't specific enough.

It was pretty bad with my son. He had a very big heroin habit. He got into some crime and he was out of control for a long time.

I was a single mother. I'd been divorced and his father went back to Europe so we were struggling for a while. I wasn't around much because I was working, and he just made the older boys at school his role models, unfortunately.

He started going out and not coming home, then things began going missing in the house. I confronted him on several occasions but it was always denial. Are you taking drugs? He'd say: 'No, of course not.'

I guess that you don't want to believe it yourself, but after a while reality sets in. That's around the time I found FDS.

It wasn't the type of thing you told a lot of friends.

I was pretty lucky in that I did talk to some friends I knew that I could trust and feel comfortable with, but you usually don't want to talk about it with people because you don't want them to think your child is a horrible person. At FDS they were all like-minded people. They would understand your stress and your shame. They didn't ever judge you.

It got better, then he went on to methadone and things got even better for a while, but then it went back again. It's like any disease—they're okay but they're never really totally cured. Times were really bad in the beginning and then they improved, and through the coping skills I learned at FDS I could put those things into practice to make life better for myself. Through doing that, it created a different type of relationship between me and my son. It got better. Of course, there were times it got worse again, but my coping skills were so much better by then that, even when it did seem hopeless, it wasn't the tragedy it used to be.

All the stories don't end in a good way all the time, but the basic thing is that the parents survive, because whenever it does go from good to bad again you need to be there to support that drug user in your family. If you don't get your own life together and make things better for yourself, you won't be able to do that.

After taking FDS's ideas on board, you do find that the relationship changes. You're not continually on their backs telling them that they have to do things— have to go to rehab. You realise that they don't have to do what you tell them and, in fact, they usually

can't because of the nature of the drug use. So, the
nagging stops and the relationship becomes better. It's
learning to make the most of the relationship you have
without deteriorating it any further.

*Maureen managed to support her son's struggle
with drugs, despite what she describes as a cloak
of secrecy and shame, and also volunteers her time,
helping others as a telephone counsellor with FDS.*

I didn't expect it to happen to him—he was quiet and
highly intelligent. He was the middle child of three. He
started using marijuana and sniffing glue. We didn't
recognise it at all because we'd had no experience with
that sort of thing whatsoever. This is going back a long
time when you were totally judged by this sort of thing
and when the only images of drug users were the ones
on television—dreadful, shocking people staggering
around in the streets, robbing people.

He left home when he was about eighteen. I knew
that things were going seriously pear-shaped for him
and I didn't want him to leave but I couldn't stop him.

I had asked him if he was using drugs but he
had denied it, and when somebody you love denies
something that is so dreadful you really want to
believe it. My husband and I were both really happy to
believe it.

When we first came to Australia, about forty years
ago, it was tough. We came with three children as

immigrants from the UK and we were so focused on establishing ourselves into society here that we might have ignored the kids a bit. But, then again, none of the other kids had these problems, so who knows what causes it?

I am pretty sure that, from the age of eighteen, when he moved out of home, he started using heroin. I think he was just as bad as the rest of them—his friends—they all egged each other on. They all shared a house together. They were all good kids from nice families and nice homes and they all went down the tubes together.

The time that my son was using has blurred into one humungous mess. Everything was so secret. You swept everything under the carpet. I was so ashamed because I could not keep him off the heroin—or any drugs for that matter. A lot of his friends were dying— overdosing. That's what happened in those days.

I, like a lot of parents who come to realise that their child is on heroin, just thought, very simplistically, that you get them into rehab and everything will be fine. That's a perfectly normal conclusion to reach. I had no idea.

But, after three days, he said what they all say— that he did not belong there and he was not like any of the people in there. He checked out, and the first thing he did was to go and score.

It was a complete nightmare. A total nightmare.

Despite all this going on, he was actually quite successful. He got a degree in mechanical engineering while he was using. His partner was a fashion

designer and still is. They had bought a place on the
Central Coast with acreage and then they both got
Hep C and they weren't well.

For a while he did everything they told him to
do—even stopped drinking.

She had a fashion show in Paris, and while she was
away my treasured son wiped out her credit cards.
Of course, that whole relationship fell through, and
my son came to live with us on our new property and
decided to get onto methadone. I had to leave home
at 5.30 a.m. every day and take him to a place where
they would give it to him because nobody nearby
would administer it—that's just the way the system
was. He had lost his licence because of drug use so he
couldn't drive himself, so after the methadone I would
drive him to where he worked.

Eventually, he got really sick of the lifestyle and
he went into rehab quite a few times and was very
unsuccessful. The heroin had quite a hold. The last
time, though, he was determined.

His lowest point? When he came to live with
us, my husband gave him a job because he had an
engineering firm. We got home from overseas and
found that he had cleaned out all our electrical goods
and that he'd crashed my husband's car. I felt great
pity for him and thought that he must have been very
sick to have done that.

My husband was very angry and I was just so
worried. One of us was going 'What have you done?'
and the other one was going 'Are you okay?'

It was FDS that turned my life around and

helped me to understand what had been going on in everyone's life. You get clouded by emotion and love and other people's opinions of you, because, apart from anything else, a lot of what you do is illegal. I mean, I took my son to Cabramatta a lot of times to get him drugs, just because it would minimise the harm that he would do to himself. He was in agony. He needed it. I don't think I told anybody that for a long time.

I tried asking for help. I phoned around and asked the doctor and they all said 'chuck him out', but I couldn't have done that to save my life. I had my attitude affirmed by Tony at FDS. My son needed very strong parental support and I was able to give it totally and unconditionally—more so after finding FDS about ten years ago.

I learned to value myself and what I had been feeling. I learned that I wasn't this dreadful parent. I learned that I was able to give this gift of caring to other people. All the stories I hear are a little bit different but they are all full of grief. Drugs destroy the lives of those around them. Not just the drug user but the people around them. I am a very emotional woman, but through FDS I have learned how to use my emotions and how not to vilify them. I've learned how to really listen to what people are saying, and I know that, for some people, I have relieved the pressure in the same way that Tony relieved it for me.

My son's drug problem went on for a long time but he doesn't use drugs now. He's had a job for three years. Could I have done anything differently to have stopped him from ever starting? I really don't think so.

I still do everything a day at a time but my story shows that recovery is definitely possible. It doesn't sound like a positive story, but to me it is, because every day that he was out and all those nights that I lay in bed wondering if he was going to come home, or if he was dead, I never thought I would see it end up like this.

Linda, 57, first suspected that her daughter Rebecca, now 32, was using drugs at the age of 14. Through the ongoing support of Family Drug Support, Linda has supported her daughter through the rehab process and now believes that Rebecca is drug-free.

My daughter was sexually abused at the age of 14 and her behaviour radically changed. I didn't know about the sexual abuse but I had suspicions that she was on drugs, although, of course, she denied it any time that I mentioned it. My thoughts were marijuana because, in my opinion, back then it was the softest option. I knew she was drinking but I didn't know to what degree.

Her school work went straight down the gurgler and she left school at fifteen. She left home at seventeen. I asked her if she was on drugs and if anything had happened in her life that had affected her which she needed help with, but all I got was denial, denial, denial—the whole way through. I even asked her if she had been sexually abused but she denied that too. But I had this child that I knew had changed and so, through process of elimination, I just asked about every possible problem.

She ended up telling us about the abuse when she was eighteen, and she didn't confirm her drug use until around the same time. By then she was living with this guy and she'd invited my husband and my daughter and me around for tea, and when we arrived, here she was in a room with half a dozen other people and they were all stoned out of their brains. From then on she never tried to deny it, she never tried to cover it up, and it was never really brought up between us. For her, it was just like, 'I'm on drugs—don't go there, Mum.'

We went through years and years and years of hell. Back then there was lots of help for the drug user but absolutely none for the family of the drug user. I tried the GPs, I tried the community health departments—there was just nothing for parents. Absolutely nothing. At the Centre Against Sexual Assault I couldn't get any help either—there was a six-month waiting list to even be seen.

Rebecca wasn't interested anyway. She'd say, 'I don't have a problem—you're the one with the problem.' She was in total denial through all of this. She thought she was in control of it.

My husband just buried his head in the sand, which is typical of a lot of men. If they can't fix the problem, they ignore it and hope that it will go away.

I can remember many a time where she would ring me up in the middle of the night, screaming her head off about this chap that she was living with, saying, 'Mum, he's going to kill me', so I'd have to jump in the car and go and rescue her from whatever situation she was in, and my husband would just roll over and say, 'You deal with it.'

After going through horrific stuff, I saw a tiny ad for a Stepping Stones program that was being offered through Family Drug Support. I went along to it and, suddenly, it was like many, many light-bulb moments all at once.

That made such a difference. When you've got a long-term problem like this, your friends and family tend to become very blasé about it all. You feel very isolated and very alone.

Rebecca then started using ice, and it was at this point that even she realised that if she didn't get out of the situation she was in, she just wasn't going to make it. My husband went over to Perth—where she was living at the time—packed her all up and brought her home. That was three years ago and she went into rehab for nine months and hasn't used since.

When my husband decided to get involved, Rebecca thought he was great. At the same time, my relationship with her went absolutely downhill. I seemed to be the one who she took all her resentment and anger out on. That's when my resentment started to grow even more, because I'd seen him sit back for so long and he was getting all the love, and yet I had been the one who had done everything and I was the one getting all the shit. I was desperate to find somewhere like FDS to help me get through it and find the strength to support her on her journey, even though she had such anger directed at me. In the end, I realised that it wasn't my husband's fault that Rebecca was going to have him as her hero and me as the bitch in the story. He was doing what I had always wanted him to do— getting involved—so I couldn't complain, really.

Rehab was hard for all of us but we got through it. Rebecca came home for a little while, but then she moved to do a twelve-month course at university and eventually she moved interstate, which is where she is living now. Our relationship is still the same, but we have more good days than bad days.

She now works for a program that teaches responsible alcohol-serving in clubs and pubs, plus she volunteers in a rehab centre and for Riding for the Disabled.

I would say that I am 95 per cent sure that she won't go back to drug use, but I don't think I would ever say it would be 100 per cent. I think it is still one day at a time.

Liz, 60, first became aware that her son, now 32, had a problem with alcohol when he was 24. The problem then extended to other drug dependencies.

His issue was originally with alcohol and he had a couple of drink-driving offences which made us aware that there was a problem. He was about 24. It just got worse and worse and he ended up giving up his job as a motor mechanic and went into rehab. After that, he moved to Newcastle to live for a while and it was while up there that I believe he began to use other drugs. There is a history of addictions right through our family. My mother was addicted to prescription medications and throughout the scattered family there are people with gambling addictions and all sorts of problems. I do think that it's a combination of genetic influence and also an environmental influence— certainly with the alcohol. As a family we're only social drinkers, but as a motor mechanic my son used to tell me that it was quite common to sit around and have a few beers at the end of his working day—not just a couple of beers but quite heavy drinking.

He started smoking cannabis and then I believe he started using speed. He looked physically different when he came home to visit: he'd lost a lot of weight and didn't have much appetite. I knew very little about drugs at that stage, but I started finding out more. If you asked too many questions he would not want to have a conversation about it. In fact, he started to avoid us.

It was probably around that time when I started to seek places that I could get help. I joined Al-Anon and I found that a great help. It was great just to be with other families who understood. I learned different ways of coping with the situation and found it really helpful. So then, when I found out that there were other drugs involved than alcohol, I looked for an organisation that would help in that way. That's how I joined Family Drug Support.

I think the fact that our mother–son relationship has been good and strong throughout this has been very important. Being angry would just be counter-productive for everybody.

My advice is to try to get as much support as you can. Just going to a support meeting once a week can let you get out all your feelings of sadness, frustration and anger. If you can actually verbalise those in a meeting, with other people who understand what you're going through, it can stop them from coming out inappropriately when you're trying to have a conversation with your son or daughter.

I'd like it to go away but who knows? I do think that things are looking up. I can see the little changes that he is trying so hard to make, but it takes a long time.

Chidem, now 27, was just 17 when her habit of smoking marijuana at weekends or at parties evolved into a heroin dependence—due to the fact that her acquaintances had been adding the white powder to her marijuana 'cones' without her knowledge. Once dependent, she soon progressed to injecting heroin and, shortly after, lost contact with her family for four years until she eventually became drug-free. She now works with Family Drug Support.

I used to be very sporty and athletic and an A-grade student, and then, when I was 17, I met someone and started smoking heroin, which soon became injecting. I dropped out of my TAFE course and left home and I just felt like I was trapped.

After many attempts at different types of detox, I couldn't find any way to get off heroin because it was all around me. I eventually went cold turkey and got off it. I started studying at TAFE for a drug and alcohol certificate IV. I needed to do some work experience somewhere and I ended up finding Family Drug Support. Since then, everything has changed. I was already clean for about two years before I met them but they have changed my life. FDS came at a vital time and gave me direction. If my parents had known that FDS existed when I was going through my worst times, they would not have gone through all that shame and stigma that goes along with having a drug user in the family. My family always had to make up lies for me at any family occasion, like Christmas or birthdays—they didn't hear from me for four years. For that four years they had no idea where I was or what I was doing. They were dying inside, every day, not knowing where their little girl was, or whether I was even still alive. Because I wasn't thinking clearly, because of the drugs, I thought that it would be better for them if I was away from them—that they would just forget about me—but obviously that wasn't the case.

One day I just decided that I wanted to go for a short visit. I was really scared—I thought Dad would be really angry and they'd lock me up or something, but Dad just said, 'Come over, everything's going to be okay, you can leave as soon as you want to and we can help you any way you need it.'

I asked them for money and they gave it to me, and then, after that, every few months I would ring them up if I needed money and they would put money in my account, so I was using my own family, really.

I went back home eventually and went cold turkey. Mum tried to talk to me a few times—to tell me about how she felt and what she was going through—but I didn't know how to deal with it all so I just wanted her to stop talking. Dad was always just a big softie and would go into his room and cry—he didn't know how to talk to me about it anyway.

Once I did my training with Family Drug Support, I realised how I could talk to them and I started questioning them in the right way so that they could finally open up and talk to me. I know it was difficult for them to talk to the person who caused them all that heartache—yet the person they still loved, despite that—but it helped a lot.

For drug users themselves, I would say 'don't ever give up'. For families—just support them—no matter what. It was a big tragedy for them to go through. Mum said that if she'd known I was dead it would have still ripped her heart out, but at least she would have known. Every night she couldn't sleep and every time there was a knock on the door she thought it was the police coming to tell them I was dead. They went through years of torture. I am so lucky that they were so strong. If my family had given up on me, I don't think I'd be here today.

Janetta, 49, found out that her daughter, Emma, now 24, was taking drugs at the age of 13.

She started to change her personality. She was a little bit more distant and began to be a little more disrespectful than she had ever been brought up to be. We couldn't figure out whether it was just adolescent behaviour or drug use. We knew something was wrong but we couldn't quite identify it. We'd ask her questions about it but she'd just deny it. The honesty just sort of dwindled away.

She got into using amphetamines and then progressed to going to nightclubs, taking Fantasy and ecstasy and then progressed to speed. She was 16 when we found that out. She was still at school and we tried to get her back on track by offering to put her in a private school—anything to try to get her to finish year eleven. We said that we would buy her a car if she did and she said 'yeah, yeah', but I think drugs had already taken over her world.

At the new school she just picked up a new lot of friends who were of the same calibre as the old friends, so we went from the frying pan into the fire. There were school kids there who were selling their younger brothers' and sisters' Ritalin—they almost had a black market for it. It was actually quite scary.

Emma was constantly yelling at me and screaming abuse at me and one day it all came to a head and that led to her having to leave that night. We gave her a choice of staying in a house with parents who actually loved and cared for her, or leaving, and she decided to leave. We didn't hear from her for about six to eight weeks and then found out she had moved into her boyfriend's house, with his parents.

We were always just hanging on to the thread of the daughter we once had, but it was all very hard to take. We didn't know of any help available so we were just trying to cope on our own. To be honest, we were a bit embarrassed about the whole thing. We didn't know the legal implications of what we were doing and it was all new to us. We hadn't dealt with drugs in our world before. We felt sure that it must have come about because we were bad parents—there's so much stigma that kids who take drugs come from parents who just don't care, but in our case that wasn't the truth at all. We did care, but we just didn't understand what we were dealing with.

We set her up in a flat, fully furnished it, and my husband got her a job where he worked. She'd have no money to buy groceries so we'd pay for that; we would pay her rent—we ended up paying for everything.

It got to the stage where our marriage was just about over and we had to try to protect our son and get things in our family back to normal, so my husband and I finally agreed that we were going to get some help for us. That was only two years ago. Now we've gone to weekly support meetings at FDS for over two years.

I think that for men it is especially great because it gives them a chance to talk in an environment where they are not judged and where they don't need to feel ashamed. For me, I had a good network of friends, but nobody really understood so FDS helped me too. Other people I knew would say 'give up on her', or, 'I don't know why you bother', but as her mother I just wanted to hang on to the child I gave birth to because you know that they're still there somewhere.

FDS helped us both by helping us to identify the fact that we were rescuing her, and also by teaching us that we could still love her and be there for her without actually financially supplying her with the money that she was obviously using to destroy her life. We thought we were saving her—paying her rent and groceries and bills—but what we were doing was actually supporting her drug use because she had all the money in the world to spend on amphetamines.

Emma moved to Melbourne and then she had a psychotic episode and ended up in a Melbourne hospital, where they recognised that she had some mental health issues. I don't know if my daughter was schizophrenic before or after she took drugs. Had I been better informed about how people react to drugs and what to expect, it might have been different, but I'll never really know.

Some people choose to go down the wrong path and all we can do is love them. I've gone from judging and having this *you can't do this with your life* attitude to just telling her, 'I don't agree with what you're doing but I love you and when you're ready not to be that person any more, I'll still be here for you.' It's brought us a lot closer together.

Amanda, 26, went from being a hard-working high-school student to injecting heroin. When the pursuit of that drug led her to the shame of criminal activity, she decided to detox. After many unsuccessful attempts, she has now been drug-free for eight years.

I don't think we had any idea. We were so naïve about what we were actually doing. My friend would be driving us back from scoring in Cabramatta and we'd be going off to sleep and she'd say, 'You've got to talk to me and keep me awake.' It's amazing we didn't die in a car accident.

I managed to keep it from my parents for quite a long time. Then, one day, I was with the girl who initially introduced it to me, at her house, and we used way too much and were in danger of overdosing, and her sister got freaked out and scared and told her parents. Then they told my parents and they also told the school about their daughter. My parents couldn't believe what was going on, and when everything blew up I actually stopped using. We weren't addicted, by any means, we were just playing a stupid game on and off.

I finished my HSC, did very well, completed school and had no contact with drugs; but then, having had such a high-pressure year with the HSC, I didn't want to go to uni, and so I moved into a relative's apartment while she was overseas and, eventually, through a girl in my workplace, ended up in a relationship with a guy who had been using for many, many years. Then I slipped back into it. Having not had an addiction, I guess I saw it as not such a big deal, but my parents were really worried.

Mum would call me and I'd be stoned so I didn't want to talk to her—probably because I was so ashamed. I know now that my parents were going through hell—that they thought that one day they were going to ring me and I would be dead—but I was oblivious to any of that at the time. The joy of heroin is that you can bury yourself in it and not have any contact with the outside world. It's like being in a dark hole.

One of the people I lived with came back from overseas with a very large amount of heroin, and so we just camped out in this house for the next however many months and developed shocking habits. It was what made it easy—I didn't have to go and break into houses and I didn't have to go and do what some of the other girls did and become a prostitute. When that supply ran out and we resorted to criminal activity, that's when I just went 'stuff this—I don't want to do this'.

I remember looking out the window one day and thinking, 'I should be starting uni now'.

The fact that I had a strong, beautiful family, a good education and came from a privileged background in comparison to a lot of the other people I was living with and using with, meant I could imagine being somewhere else. That's when the whole process of trying to get clean really began. It was a reasonably long one—trying to go cold turkey and doing doctor-supported detoxes.

I went home to Mum and Dad at one stage and managed to detox there. I got a job and was trying to show them and myself that I could do this, but then I slipped back in. Because my younger sister was doing her HSC, they just couldn't have me in the house. They made it very clear. My father was always very angry about the situation and my mother was as understanding as she could be, and I think that's around the time that they engaged with Family Drug Support. That was the only place they could go.

My mum got me to go and get some counselling with Tony, and my parents remained in contact with FDS as I went through the process of going in and out of using, and then, eventually, going on the methadone program.

Now that I am a mother, I understand entirely what my own mum went through. If my own daughter ever ended up in a similar situation I would be absolutely devastated and I wouldn't give up—and my mum didn't either. She tried her best and she kept being pushed away, but she was still so supportive. Mum was right beside me at the doctor's when I detoxed.

I would say that, after their contact with Tony and FDS, my parents did become more understanding and really tried to help me work through it—even when it was really hard.

That was eight years ago. I think it's something that they'd rather forget. I became someone unrecognisable then. I completely lost myself. I was no longer Amanda.

We do talk about it every now and then—we haven't tried to bury it—but I can tell that they're glad it's over. My relationship with my mum now is great. I'm on the phone to my mother at least once or twice a week—just to have a friendly chat. She's an incredible support to me, and I understand my dad a lot better than I did before too. I have an incredibly tight, honest relationship with both my parents.

My life is completely different now. I have completed two uni degrees and I am a qualified social worker. I have a beautiful seven-year-old daughter who is my life, and an amazing partner. My life now is exactly where I want it to be.

With the help of FDS, Leila, 48, has supported her brother, Joseph, through his drug dependency. Cultural differences have added problems to an already challenging situation, but Leila feels confident that her brother will eventually be drug-free.

He told us the day after my fortieth birthday party—just came out and said, 'I've been using drugs and I need help.' I don't think he realised how serious the problem was, but he'd had a friend who had died from a heroin overdose and so I think there was a bit of fear.

We had all been aware that he had been smoking some cannabis but it really did come as a complete shock that he had a heroin problem. He was about eighteen.

I think it was quite a typical reaction from my parents—Mum kept saying that she knew something was wrong, and Dad's reaction was, 'Oh well, that's fine—he'll get over this very quickly.' It was complete denial about how serious the problem was, but a relief that at least it was out in the open.

My brother seemed to spiral down quite badly after telling the family. At that stage he had just been smoking heroin but then he started injecting, which really freaked everyone out. My father initially went through the stages of wanting to kick him out—and my other brother did too—and it was the women in the family who kept saying 'no, no'.

I used to work in community health so we looked for help very quickly. My sister knew someone who had been in contact with Family Drug Support and it was Tony who was able to help us all. Everyone was throwing blame around—Mum was blaming Dad, Dad was blaming Mum, they were both blaming my sister, and when we should have been pulling together it was all coming apart. There was a great deal of anger. FDS helped educate my mother, mainly. We knew that if we could get her to understand, then the family had a chance of getting through this.

I think that there was a lot of shame and guilt, which was exacerbated by our culture because, in our culture, to belong is a very big part of life, and when you have a secret like this and it is perceived as shame on the family—not just the individual involved—you can become ostracised.

My father still cannot talk about it—even today—but my mother got more strength and she does have a close group of friends and family that she talks to.

My brother is on methadone and he seems to be doing well. He has a very isolated life but he has held down a job for two and a half years, which is great. I think he may be using some drugs but I'm not sure what. He still lives with my parents and has had periods where he has gone in and out of rehab—there isn't anything he hasn't tried over the last eight years.

I think the key things that FDS teaches are 'hold on and let go'. It's how you continue to love them, but don't accept what they're doing. FDS helps to remind you to continue to maintain the links with your loved one, no matter how angry or disappointed you are, and that the family needs to pull together—not tear apart.

I send my brother little things in the mail every few months—just reminding him of how far he's come and how proud we are of him that he is still trying. He's doing really well. He's now managing a team of six people at work and I feel confident that he will change and get better.

Even my father, who couldn't talk about it without crying, now feels confident that he will get better. He might not get there in the time that we want him to, but he will get there eventually.

CHAPTER 9

Harm Minimisation Saves Lives

Harm minimisation:
The limiting of harm that is done to both the individual and to the community, resulting from the use of tobacco and other drugs.

You might have seen the topic of harm minimisation written about in magazines and newspapers, or heard it talked about on television or radio news reports. Harm minimisation has been on the National Drug Strategy since 1985—although from recent political rhetoric you might not think so. It is the philosophical approach used by most drug and alcohol services in Australia today—something I believe to be a very practical response to drug issues. I feel that the thinking behind it is realistic and helpful and acknowledges the impact of drugs and alcohol on both the individual and the wider community. Unfortunately, though, because the concept of harm minimisation is one which challenges the insular nature of misconceptions about drugs and the people who use them, it is still a response that a large number of people see as frightening.

Harm minimisation should not scare you. If applied to your own situation, it may help save the life of the drug user in your own life.

Dr Alex Wodak explained the philosophy wonderfully in his foreword to this book, saying: 'Harm minimisation is based on the understanding that drug dependence is often a relapsing condition and that caring for drug users must focus first and foremost on keeping them alive. After all, where there is life, there is hope.'

And I agree. I realise that some of the issues around harm minimisation may be difficult for many people to grasp—the idea that legalising the very drugs that can clearly cause so much harm could possibly be a solution—but I do believe that it needs to be explored. When discussing harm minimisation and the legalisation of drugs in the same breath, it is important to remember that harm minimisation is not about the moral sanctioning of drug use and certainly not about encouraging or promoting drug use to young people who have never been involved with drugs.

Where there is life, though, as Dr Wodak said, there truly is hope, and if keeping drug users alive involves initiatives such as providing sterile injection equipment and safer places to inject, replacing the unknown elements of street drugs with similar, controlled substances, and ensuring the wide-spread distribution of honest, accurate safety and drug management-related information to drug users, then I believe it makes sense.

When we first started FDS, while lip service was paid to harm minimisation, both state and federal governments shied away from reforms like injecting centres. I think everyone just wanted to maintain the status quo and not be the one to step out on his or her own to propose anything that could be viewed as controversial. So, even though there were recommendations from a lot of experts in the field, both the government of New South Wales, where I live, and the federal government were very hesitant to do anything to get the ball rolling. However, across Australia, the state governments and Dr Wooldridge, representing the Commonwealth, did eventually agree to a heroin prescription trial and announced that it was going to go ahead.

According to the plans, it was going to be a three-phase trial, similar to the Swiss model that had been working quite well since 1994, and there were many people who were very excited about the potential outcomes—until Prime Minister Howard intervened and objected. This was in August 1997, very shortly after the launch of FDS, and I was very publicly vocal in my opposition to the prime minister, who then put together a task force and came up with his 'tough on drugs' strategy.

Around the same time, the NSW government were making their own response to the idea of injecting facilities. I gave evidence at an Upper House inquiry—chaired by Ann Symonds who eventually became chairperson of FDS—along with a lot of other people, and when you read through that report, the evidence for injecting facilities is just overwhelming. I think that there were one or two objections from people on moral grounds, and a couple of businesses in Kings Cross objected because, I suppose, of the 'not in my backyard' mentality, but, overwhelmingly, the evidence in favour of the initiative was positive. Despite the report being positive about the introduction of such facilities the committee voted against introducing them in NSW. I was advocating these kinds of reforms pretty strongly at that time, and I decided to go to the International Harm Reduction Conference in Geneva in 1998 and take the opportunity to go and visit first-hand such facilities—both the injecting facilities and the heroin prescription trials. I guess I had always had this attitude that if I was shown to the contrary, I would be prepared to change my views, so I must admit that I went with a little bit of trepidation—given that I had been so vocal about my opinions. I didn't need to worry. The end result was that, having seen them in action for myself, I came back a strong supporter—convinced that, done carefully, the lives of many young Australians could be saved.

I visited facilities in Geneva and Beme—facilities that were located in commercial areas and shopping areas and even residential areas. The Swiss had taken everything in their stride, and, from what I could understand, there was no apparent negative response whatsoever. Prior to this initiative there had been very big problems with a lot of public use of drugs, as well as careless discarding of drug-related implements, and so both the government and the public had seen that the changes had actually brought about enormous benefits—not just to the individuals directly involved but also to the broader community. The injecting facility wasn't just a place for drug users to gather and inject, but a place to get food, free of charge, and receive information and advice about drug using, health checks and access to counsellors. It was a place where they could actually spend a lot of time and be exposed to social workers—a place where there were many, many positives.

These trials showed that, for people on heroin prescription, everything in their lives improves. Housing, health, employment, relationships—it all improves. During the process of improvement and enrichment, lives can be saved because drug use is carefully monitored. Because the users are no longer focused on the logistics of getting heroin each and every day, they have more time and energy to think about other things—which often includes the idea of getting themselves off the drug. Figures show that as many of the participants appear to subsequently give up heroin as would have done in rehab. The three big damages of heroin use are death, disease and crime. If you legalise heroin, I believe that you get rid of those three. If it can save the life of even one young person—someone's son, daughter, sister, brother— surely it is worth it.

There is, of course, still the dependency issue, which, although it seems like a huge thing left to deal with, may also become less problematic. It has been shown that people can function—often quite highly—while dependent. Even with the way things are in Australia today, with the way methadone is distributed, it has been proven that people can use that every day and still function as active members of society—holding down jobs, studying, and being part of happy, united families.

I came back from Switzerland more determined than ever that we needed something similar in Australia, and for the next few months after that there were underground meetings held in Kings Cross—meetings attended by doctors, nurses, social workers, clergymen and myself representing Family Drug Support—where it was decided that we would, as an act of civil disobedience, open an injecting facility. Reverend Ray Richmond, who was the pastor of Wayside Chapel, very bravely offered the chapel as the venue. We were about to do that at the beginning of 1999 and then Bob Carr announced the Drug Summit, so there was a lot of discussion about whether we should go ahead with the idea and if it would have a positive or negative influence on the Drug Summit. As it happened, we decided to go ahead and open it before the Drug Summit, and I believe that it turned out to be a key element in the eventual decision to have an injecting centre in New South Wales. It was a short-lived experiment that was only open two or three hours a day for about nine days before it was eventually closed down, but it did bring a lot of attention to the issue. We called it the 'Tolerance Room'.

There were calls from certain people, such as Reverend Fred Nile (Leader of the Christian Democratic Party and head of the Festival of Light) and some politicians, that those involved should be jailed, and, in fact, Reverend Ray Richmond was arrested, along with some drug users who were using the facility at the time. Thankfully, the charges were later thrown out of court, but the topic was put firmly on the agenda for the Summit.

Now, after many trials and tribulations and objections, the centre is well-ensconced in the Kings Cross area and, from what I have seen and heard, the majority of residents agree that it is a positive thing. I am very proud that a lot of FDS people were involved in that, and hope that it is just one step towards further implementation of harm minimisation initiatives across Australia. If it saves just one life—perhaps the life of your loved one—isn't it the right thing?

I believe that helping a parent or other family member avoid the problems associated with drug use is not so much about telling people to watch out for a checklist of warning signs that they might recognise in their own family member, but that we have to, as a whole society, start understanding what drugs are all about. The first step towards harm minimisation is ensuring that we open up communication and learn to talk about drug-related issues honestly—in the media, in the home and in the classroom.

We have to start accepting what kids are doing and learn how to better manage the potential consequences, rather than merely lecturing them with a zero-tolerance mindset. We need to try to understand them. As any parent surely knows, you can advise them, over and over again, not to do it, but that is not always going to make the difference. In fact, nagging and lecturing may even inch them closer towards the very thing you want them to avoid. After all, in the case of young people, some form of rebellion against what were once the guiding forces in their lives is a natural part of growing up. Rather than bombard them with messages of 'just say no', 'don't ever do it', 'you had better not even think about trying it', or, 'if I ever find out you did you'll be in so much trouble', what you need to tell them is that if they do find themselves in trouble they should come to you—that they can trust you.

Some people think that legalisation is the wrong approach and that it's giving young people carte blanche to behave badly, but I don't agree. I don't believe that legalisation of drugs would inspire a lot of people to suddenly take them. There would still be a lot of people—the majority—who never would. I don't think there would be any increase in drug use.

Obviously, the way it is handled is critical. If drugs are suddenly sold behind the counter in Coles supermarkets and marketers spend huge sums of money on advertising campaigns that encourage people to try the product, then, yes, of course there would be an increase in the numbers of drug users. Personally, just as has been done with cigarettes, I would ban all drug-related advertising—alcohol included. Having control of the manufacture and distribution would mean that the strength of the products was strictly monitored and it would obviously be a lot safer. If you were a drug user, you could then buy it legally without the stigma of having committed a crime and without having to pay the huge prices that lead some drug users to theft and prostitution. Managing it is not the same as promoting it.

I want to make it clear that, while I do not want to be an advocate for legalisation, I do believe that the time for society to take a pragmatic view of this issue is long overdue.

Playing your own part in harm-minimisation philosophies does not have to involve political lobbying or protest. Applying harm-minimisation principles to your own family situation is about minimising risks to what is already a risky existence—the life of a drug user. By taking some precautions, I firmly believe that lives can be saved.

DEVELOP A FAMILY CONTINGENCY PLAN

The discovery that someone you love is using drugs causes a lot of anxiety and fear about what may happen. Common fears include:

- death by overdose
- contraction of a blood-borne virus—HIV or Hepatitis
- worries that the drug user's activities will lead to arrest, conviction or jail
- other family members leaving home because of the behaviour of the drug user
- ill health of the drug user or another family member— brought on by stress related to the concerns about the drug user
- conflict within the family escalating out of control with disastrous consequences
- increased mental-illness issues
- the breakdown of the family due to the flow-on effect of problems related to the drug user
- violence

- things never getting better
- children being born into uncertain or difficult situations
- property damage.

Some things families are fearful about will not occur—some may. Because of the daily chaos and trauma they deal with, families very rarely make practical contingency plans to counter some of the possible events. For some people still in the denial stage, the idea of having such plans may be seen as a resignation that there really is a problem—a reality that they are still happier avoiding. It is, though, both useful and practical to have an easily accessible list of relevant telephone numbers, should it be needed. Having such a list does not mean that negative things will happen—it is simply about being prepared in case they do. The list should contain services available in your local community and detail both phone numbers and addresses, where applicable. Include:

- local hospital and other emergency numbers
- the Mental Health Crisis Team
- Family Drug Support
- Alcohol and Drug Information Service
- the police
- neighbours who can intervene quickly in an emergency—whether that means helping you directly, or looking after other family members such as young children, or the elderly, if your urgent attention is needed elsewhere
- a solicitor
- a counsellor
- friends to talk to
- needle and syringe services
- a drug-user group.

Zero tolerance clearly does not work. It hasn't worked in the United States, where their drug problems are well known. Harm minimisation is really just a logical extension of the recognition that human beings will continue to do dangerous things—a way to ensure that we, as a society, must endeavour to keep that damage to a minimum.

Maureen's son, now 44, had a long-term drug problem that began when he was a teenager. She believes that better education about drugs, combined with legalisation of drugs, could save the lives of many existing drug users—and the lives of future generations.

I really believe that drugs should be legalised because so many of the young people do use them and they don't know how to use them safely. They need to be better educated about drug use.

I think a mum should have the legality of being able to say to their children, 'If you are going to use an ecstasy tablet, make sure it is a safe one.'

Instead, mums have to judge whether their children are using ecstasy or whatever, and then just trust to luck what they're actually taking. I think that is so unfair—especially when alcohol is legal. So much money is made out of drugs. So many people are benefiting from other people's misery. To me that is completely and utterly wrong.

Drug use is so clever. It's so secretive and it's masked so well. Living by example does not work on its own. It seems a rotten world out there at the moment but you can be prepared. You have to be informed.

When you lose a child, it is the hardest grief of all. When you lose a child to drugs, you carry extra burdens. If Australia had had the heroin trial when it was first proposed, we could have at least determined, first-hand, whether it was useful to give people prescribed heroin. Now, it is unknown. Will it happen again? In the current political climate, unfortunately, I doubt it, although I do hope there comes a time when governments are far-sighted enough to realise that it could be worth giving it a try. As our young people continue to die, it is clear that what is happening now is not the best answer.

The concept of harm reduction and minimisation for drug users was born in 1986 with the realisation that the HIV virus was being spread through the sharing of syringes among heroin-injecting users. To reduce the risk of an increase in AIDS cases, Australia took a bold step and led the world in the availability and distribution of new syringes to injecting drug users. As a result, Australia now has the lowest incidence of HIV among injecting drug users in the world—less than 2 per cent, compared to figures of up to 90 per cent in some other countries.

While the availability of clean syringes has halted the spread of HIV infection, though, it has not halted the spread of Hepatitis C (HCV) infection. This is because the HCV virus is much more easily picked up from any sort of blood contact. There are several harm reduction strategies, in addition to clean syringes, that should be followed to reduce the risk of HCV and other disease transmission. Some strategies also reduce other health risks associated with injecting drug use such as vein care, sexual and gynaecological health and dental and psychological care.

HARM MINIMISATION AND DRUG-TAKING BEHAVIOUR

While I believe that a simplistic 'just say no' approach to education has not worked and does not take into consideration the risk-taking nature of some young people, it is obvious that the best way to avoid drug problems is not to start using them. Other ways to minimise or reduce the harms associated with drug-taking are to develop controls in relation to the use and quality of particular substances. This idea is well known in relation to controlling legal drugs such as alcohol, tobacco and prescription drugs—e.g. the idea of a standard drink or a daily medication dose that comes with a warning label advising users to take just a measured amount and not exceed this over a 24-hour period. Quality controls regulate the manufacturing process of wine, spirits, beer and pharmaceuticals to ensure they have the same percentage ingredients by volume in each bottle, can or tablet produced. A well-known tobacco and alcohol regulation is that it must not be sold to people younger than 18 years.

For people who are having difficulties with drug-taking behaviour, options are:

- to quit, give up their drug behaviour and maintain ongoing abstinence from the drug
- to reduce or cut down the drug behaviour and control its use
- to continue to use but to do so as safely as possible
- to give up some drugs but to continue taking others, e.g. stop taking heroin, but keep smoking cannabis.

Goals tend to change over time in incremental steps and success that builds on success is more sustainable.

Most of us have probably met a reformed or reforming smoker who has tried some or all of the above. Perhaps they have kept smoking but smoked cigarettes with a lower nicotine level. Perhaps they have cut down the number of cigarettes smoked in a 24-hour period. They may have even tried using nicotine gum or patches to reduce cigarette cravings, or they may have simply gone 'cold turkey' and remained abstinent— sometimes lapsing a few times before they managed to kick the habit for good. With illicit substances, however, we are unable to use quality-control standards or regulatory measures apart from efforts to reduce availability (supply) and education to reduce usage (demand). Our society's experiences in dealing with people affected by legal drugs tells us that going from detoxification to abstinence is not a quick process and that we also need measures that will control harm for the public, e.g. no smoking in the workplace and, most recently, in clubs and pubs. In these circumstances, harm-minimisation policies work with the reality of the situation—not necessarily the ideal that we wish for.

Likewise, with illicit drug use, other options are also needed, such as:

- more knowledge and research with information on various drug effects, particularly when drugs are combined
- treatment programs that are flexible and specifically designed with the individual in mind
- controlled drug use as an option for opiate (heroin) dependence, through use of substitute prescription medi- cation such as methadone or buprenorphine
- needle and syringe programs that provide drug and sexual health education, referral and provision of sterile injecting equipment and condoms.

Unfortunately, there are still many myths and misconceptions about drugs and drug users and this continues to perpetuate the shame and stigma experienced by families. The impact of this is that many families will struggle on in secret, ashamed and afraid to ask for help. A lack of awareness that a drug problem is a health issue rather than an issue of eroded morality or a result of weakness of character can contribute to the silent turmoil that families dealing with these issues live in. Harm minimisation is a practical response to drug issues and one which challenges the insular nature of such misconceptions. It is realistic and practical and acknowledges the impact of drugs and alcohol on the individual and the wider community.

INJECTING DRUGS—A GUIDE TO HARM MINIMISATION FOR USERS

- Never use drugs alone. The majority of drug users will overdose at least once and a companion can call for help in the event of an overdose.
- Do not inject in a public toilet because of the risk of infection, and, in the case of overdose, people will not be able to get access to give help.
- Use a supervised injecting room if one is available.
- Blood-borne viruses can be spread from one person to another with even the slightest blood contact. When injecting drugs maintain a clear space around you so that you do not come into contact with any other person.
- Regular drug use may be more harmful than occasional use. The risks of drug use increase as the quantity of drug used increases.
- Regular drug use increases the chance that a person will become involved in criminal activities.

- Don't plan to have a few drinks or get intoxicated before using drugs as this increases the chance of risk-taking behaviour.
- If you use drugs, think of other people and do not drive or use firearms. You are at risk of injury if you drive or ride a bike, operate machinery, go swimming or take part in active or dangerous sports.
- Use drugs in a safe place, not near railway lines or busy roads.
- Use of some drugs will encourage sexual activity . . . practise safe sex at all times.
- Ulcers and damaged veins and skin infections need medical treatment. Sudden onset of fever with tiredness and lack of energy may be due to infection and needs urgent medical attention.
- Tell the doctor what you have been injecting.
- Try to have breakfast and at least one decent meal every day.
- Regular exercise, sports activity or weight training will help to keep your body healthy.
- Tobacco, alcohol, illicit or prescription drugs can all be dangerous during pregnancy. Their use can result in pre-term babies, underweight and underdeveloped babies as well as deformities. If you become pregnant while using drugs, contact your local hospital as soon as possible for advice.
- Do you feel relaxed and contented when you use drugs but tense and unhappy when the effect wears off? Perhaps, as a short-term measure, your doctor could prescribe something that reduces the tension so that you can enjoy a feeling of wellbeing.
- Drug use can cause financial problems for the user.

HARM MINIMISATION—A GUIDE FOR PARENTS

Be informed

Parents whose children have died due to drug-taking often say in hindsight, 'If only I'd known then what I know now.' While it may seem that your child gets all their information and values from their peers, research shows that they actually fall back on the values and attitudes of their family and parents more than may appear obvious at first. Don't preach, just try to open a discussion or leave information around the house.

Give them accurate information

Your local Community Health Centre should have a range of information, and you can also use the information from this book or the fact sheets available at our website at www.fds.org.au or www.yds.org.au.

Talk to their friends (even those you may consider a bad influence)

Don't be afraid to talk to their friends. By alienating the peer group they have chosen, no matter how much you disapprove, you will also alienate them. Peer pressure can increase the likelihood of having unprotected sex, using drugs and alcohol, and exposure to other risky behaviour. The most obvious one is driving and alcohol—most road fatalities have alcohol as a factor.

Getting into fights, stealing or being involved in daring acts like hanging off trains can be common behaviour when drugs are combined, e.g. alcohol, coke, speed, uppers, dope and prescription drugs. This is especially so with younger teenagers and party drugs such as ecstasy, acid and prescription drugs, and, of course, alcohol.

Encourage them to take a phone card linked to your home phone number. Stress the importance of them being able to get home safely either by calling a cab, which you can pay for on arrival, or that you will collect them and give them a lift home.

Make sure your child's friends are aware of the dangers of drug use, safe drug-use procedures, and that they recognise overdose symptoms and act quickly.

It is important that if anyone in the group is physically distressed that friends stay with them and care for them while not hesitating to get medical help or an ambulance if necessary. An untreated overdose or adverse reaction can be fatal if unattended to.

Make sure the group of friends are aware that:

- Mixing drugs and especially mixing drugs and alcohol is EXREMELY dangerous.
- Signs of a bad reaction to drugs should not be ignored and it is crucial to call an ambulance immediately.
- Police need not always be involved, and, even if they are, their prime concern is health and safety.
- Information must be provided as to what has been taken so that treatment can be administered effectively and immediately.
- It is better to deal with an unpleasant situation than for someone to suffer brain damage or death.

Promote responsibility

- Introduce the idea of one member of the group remaining sober or clean when out partying. Not only can they be the 'voice of reason', but they can also be aware of signs of overdose or reactions to any drugs being used. They will be more likely to be responsible for seeking help and calling an ambulance if necessary.

- Encourage responsible drug and alcohol use. This will ensure that the person looks after their own health and also shows concern for the people around them. For injecting drug users, sterile conditions and correct disposal practices are a must, especially if there are younger siblings or children in the home. The same responsibilities apply to leaving pills or powders around, which can be lethal should young curious children come across them.
- Promote safe sex. This may be even more important for drug users than anyone else. Encourage them to ALWAYS use condoms. Loss of inhibition and control can cause people to do things that they would never normally do— including having unprotected sex.
- Promote ways to maintain general health. Drug and alcohol use reduces the body's ability to use vitamins and minerals and often suppresses the appetite. Partying in smoke-filled rooms, prolonged alcohol use and side effects of other drugs all contribute to overall poor health.

Due to large financial expenditure on drugs, users often have less money to spend on food. As a result, people's immunity to disease can be lowered and they may have colds and flu more often, as well as specific problems associated with the way particular drugs are taken, e.g. nasal problems with snorting, vein problems with injecting drug users, chronic constipation with opiate use. A diet that is low in fast food and high in fresh fruit and vegetables will help, as will drinking plenty of water and juice. Whenever you can, encourage your child to have healthy food and take a vitamin or mineral supplement as well as exercise. Going for a walk to the beach or the park every so often can also be helpful. Health is obviously crucially important if your drug user is female and pregnant. If your child is living on the streets, encourage them to eat freely available good food such as that accessable at the Hare Krishna temples and at many soup kitchens.

Listen, listen, listen and listen . . .

One of the things that parents often tell FDS is that when they reflect on what happened, they only heard what they wanted to hear, rather than what was happening in reality. Our natural instinct is to deny reality. This is a very dangerous instinct that we need to challenge. What we all need is to be listened to. Listening means suspending your thoughts and judgements and focusing on what the other person is telling you.

Help them be less chaotic and more organised

Provide assistance so that they are able and equipped to deal with the rules of bureaucracy. Being disorganised and under the influence of drugs may impact on their ability to maintain an income, stay out of court or jail, and keep in employment. For you, this may mean doing practical things like:

- reminding them about dates to see the parole officer, ensuring they check in, in accordance with their bail conditions, reminding them to ring treatment services
- giving them a lift or bus and train fares to keep appointments
- buying them a prepaid phone card so you can contact each other
- buying them some reasonable clothes: having to live in tattered clothes does nothing for a person's self-esteem or for their image when dealing with bureaucratic systems.

The most harm—overdose

This is, of course, the BIG FEAR for parents, but it's not as common as you may think. Overdose risk is increased when:

- the person is alone
- they have taken a different amount of a drug to what they are used to
- they have reduced or stopped using but have lapsed back into drug-taking again
- they are combining different drugs, particularly alcohol, illicit drugs and/or prescription drugs such as benzo-diazepines.

Hopefully, it will never happen to you, but by being prepared you could make a difference. Basic first-aid skills (resuscitation training) and, as mentioned earlier, a list of relevant support services or medical centres could help. Remember, applying the principles of harm minimisation into your own experience does not make you an advocate for drug use. It may, though, give your loved one their best chance at survival.

∗ The definition of harm minimisation used at the start of this chapter comes from *Nurses Strategic Plan: A Teaching Kit for Nurses* (1994) by Reid, Powell and Brown.

CHAPTER 10

Bereavement

When it comes to talking about the possible ramifications of alcohol misuse and drug dependency, bereavement is not a topic that many family members want to acknowledge. That, of course, is understandable. I hope that one message you have taken from this book is one of hope and positivity—a glimpse that life can get better.

While that is true for many people, though, there are, very sadly, some for whom such positivity does not seem possible. They are the family members who, like me, lose their beloved child, parent, or sibling forever to drugs.

Over my years with FDS, I have seen a lot of people suffer through bereavement and I see them fit into three categories:

The first way of grieving is when people act like the overdose death never happened and as if the child and all memories of that child have been erased from the family's history. The dead person is not talked about, any family photos on display are removed and packed away, and conversations about the person are avoided and discouraged. It is something that I have seen a lot of fathers do, and when it comes to dealing with bereavement and the complexity of grief, it is, without a doubt, the most harmful, unhealthy way to 'cope'. It can also lead to alienation and/or conflict as the other parent, often, is left wanting acknowledgement.

The second way is that ten, fifteen, or more years later, the family members are still grieving as they did on the first day of their loved one's death—they just haven't moved on at all. That, too, is unhealthy and does not allow the family members left to truly move on and celebrate the other positive things that may happen in their lives. When parents do it, as their way of dealing with the dreadful loss of a son or daughter, it impacts negatively on the other siblings still living and can also have disastrous consequences for the relationship between the mother and father, who remain stuck in the void of loss and sadness.

Sad as it may seem on the surface, the healthiest form of grieving is where there is still some pain and obvious loss—where there has been a definite ritual to say goodbye and the dead family member is remembered . . . always. It is reasonable and natural for that remembering to be done with sadness, but it shouldn't stop the family from living.

I often ask families who are stuck in deep grief, 'What would your child have wanted you to do?' Their response is usually, 'He would want us to remember him—especially the good times—but not be crippled.'

Colette, 54, lost her son, Ronnie, four years ago, when he was just 27. Like Damien Trimingham, Ronnie seemed to be on the road to recovery and succumbed to an overdose after not using as regularly as he once did.

Ronnie started drinking at an early age. He was troublesome throughout his childhood—he started stealing and lying to me—and I tried to do the best I could as a single mother, but I knew that there was a lot of emotional pain behind it all. He was about 15 at this stage and I moved with him back to Ireland, thinking that perhaps he would be able to connect with other members of the family and he would be happier. Instead, it had the opposite effect. Drugs are so easily accessible in Dublin and so from drinking he was introduced to ecstasy and cannabis.

He met a young girl and really fell in love and she had two children with Ronnie, but that whole relationship was so filled with turmoil because of what was now his drug addiction. He got very sick and we found out that he was suffering from epilepsy, and he told me the reason was because, in his words, he had 'fried his brain'. It was only then that I found out he had been using heroin too. The mental and physical deterioration, I believe, were all caused by his drug use.

He turned into this horrible person I didn't recognise. There were all the signs of drug use—lying, stealing, violent outbursts, hallucinations and paranoia. His self-hatred got worse—he was a complete mess. When people use drugs they leave themselves open to so many things—drugs that are laced with anything, and the different people that they mix with on the streets. It's a very worrying thing.

I didn't have anyone to turn to for support, really. I come from a conservative, religious family, and if you're not working and you're not pulling your weight then you're not seen as a worthwhile person so I was advised to get rid of him. People said, 'He's not worth it—he's causing you trouble', and 'Look what he's doing to you.' I don't blame my parents for looking at it that way—that's what they believed and that's what I did.

Ronnie lived out in a field and then I thought, 'This is my son.' I wouldn't have allowed a dog to live like that, and while he was away from me—living outside— I didn't know where he was. Not only was I worried about him but I was thinking about other people too. If living like that was forcing him to steal from someone else, or if he got in a car and drove and killed someone, I couldn't have lived with it, so I changed my viewpoint and I didn't turn him away again.

In Dublin there was no sympathy or understanding at all—no detox units in the hospitals and no real support for the drug user or the family. Ronnie tried to detox 'cold turkey' and I tried to help him through that, because by then I had realised that if I was helping him, I was actually helping myself too. He ended up on this merry-go-round of getting a job to get money, using it for drug use, losing his job, then getting a job, using money for drug use, and

losing the job again. In all of this, though, I still saw
my son. I didn't want to give up. We did find a type of
family drug support in Dublin eventually—nothing
like the Family Drug Support here—that was helpful.
It was in a little room on top of a garage, which was so
undignified, but the people there were absolute angels.

Watching Ronnie go through detox was one of the
worst things I had ever experienced—him feeling sick
and having hallucinations—but even then you're naïve
and you think 'once they go through detox, that will
be it', but it's not. Two weeks later he was back on the
drugs again. He got through a second five-day detox,
but it wasn't long after that he was back using again.
It doesn't happen overnight—not at all. I knew one
woman in my area—and it was not a bad area—who
had five children and four had died from drugs. She
was waiting on the fifth.

I knew that we were at our limit there, and that if
we came back to Australia, Ronnie would have a much
better chance at survival. We sold up everything and
came back. It was a lot easier to get Ronnie into rehab
here than it had been in Ireland and he seemed to be
doing really well. He went into Odyssey House and
they detoxed him with no pain, and then he went into
their program—which I thought was a major thing—
but then he left it.

Ronnie and I had always said to each other that,
once we got through the drugs thing, we would both
do a course to become volunteers and try to give back
to the community to help others—just because we
had learned so much from the experience. So, when

he died, I felt like I still needed to do that. That's what led me to find FDS. I rang Tony and he really helped me a lot. I was able to talk to him openly about my son's death and the experiences I'd had. I had felt so guilty and responsible. I was depressed and, to be honest, I didn't want to carry on my life. Tony had been through a very similar experience and so he understood. He told me that we do the best we can with what we know at the time. To get that reassurance and to hear those words made me very happy. I did do the best I could—I really did help my son—but hearing that from someone else was very important. I am fulfilling what was a vision that both Ronnie and I wanted to do, so while I am helping with FDS today, being a volunteer, it makes me feel very close to my son. Parents often feel that they have nobody to turn to. Friends and families often isolate them, and sometimes the shame and stigma is so great, it makes it very difficult to cope. Personally, for me, it's still very difficult. To lose a child before we go—it just doesn't work. I think I cried morning, noon and night for about a year.

I was in total shock through the funeral. I just couldn't believe it—he was really making it. He almost got there. Those young people who have rehabilitated and who are making it—they're the ones who really are at risk because the drug is out of their body but they still haven't really coped with saying 'no' and fighting the cravings, so if they take it one more time, there's a possibility that they can OD and die, which is exactly what happened to my son.

There is not enough education out there for young people and parents—to teach drug users and parents to try to find an environment where there is harm minimisation and some level of safety. That they don't have to die. In coping with my own bereavement, I have found out so much information and just wish that I'd had it all before and that I could have implemented it. Sometimes I wonder, if I had known all the things I know now, whether Ronnie might still be alive, but I'll never know. When I lived in Ireland, I had lost hope, but when I came out to Australia with him, there was, again, some hope. My bereavement will never go away, but it will get easier. Today, it's one day at a time. That's all.

For parents watching a child go through rehab or detox, I would say to keep an extra close eye on them. They should learn as much as they can about drugs and what they do to someone. The more you know, the better, I think. Get as much information as you can and then find a non-judgemental, empathetic, holistic approach to working through the problem. For the drug addict, they should also have more education so that they know when they are at the vital point of making it through.

After progressing from marijuana to injecting a variety of drugs, Caroline's son, Kane, passed away in 2002. He was 27.

Kane was about sixteen and was drinking like normal sixteen-year-olds drink, then he started smoking marijuana very heavily and that caused depression. He smoked marijuana for a lot of years and then he started using amphetamines to bring himself out of the depression that the marijuana had caused. Then he started using ice. This was over a ten-year period.

We sort of figured it out along the way, and every now and then he would go to doctors and put his hand up for help and then he'd go secretive again—it was very up and down. It's hard to say when he was being honest and when he wasn't.

I didn't find out about FDS until after Kane had died. I'd rung up all the helplines and they gave me information, but they didn't give me any help. I knew every street name of every drug and what they did to your body, but they also told me to kick him out, that he had to hit rock bottom and put his own hand up for help. If I had kicked my son out and done tough love like they suggested, I would have lost Kane years before I did. There was no way I could have done that. He was my child. He was in need and he needed my help. I stuck to him like glue.

It really did nearly destroy our family, because my husband—Kane's stepdad—wanted to take the hard line, and I wanted to look after him. Part of what Tony does for families who find FDS is to keep families together. That's so important.

I had another son—a 12-year-old—and there were times when Kane was so psychotic on ice that I could not bring my little boy home from school, and I'd have to ring another mother and ask them to take him home to their house just so he wouldn't see it. Kane never hurt anybody—he never stole and he never went to jail—but he was psychotic and paranoid. It was becoming dangerous to have him around.

In the end I did have to say, 'You have to get help or you can't come back here.' That nearly killed me, but Kane understood. He felt great shame and he didn't want to expose us to that either, so he went and lived with this woman who eventually had his child— my grandson—and she was a user too. From that point on he just declined.

He knew that she was four months pregnant and he was excited about the baby. He thought this baby would turn him around, but he knew that she had major drug problems—she'd already had two children taken off her—so he was worried about the baby. He rang me on the Friday before he died and told me he was going into detox. He said: 'She's not going to be able to look after this baby and I've got to get myself right to look after it.'

I went and picked him up and drove him in and then I rang the detox place on the Sunday to see how he was going and he'd left. He came to see me at work on Monday because I had his cash card and he needed money and he looked great. He was smiling and he looked healthy and I told him: 'You look great.'

I said, 'Just get well, Kane, that's all I want.' And he said, 'I'm trying, Mum.'

He died that night.

I will never know exactly what happened. There had been some sort of altercation because he had an abrasion on his head. This person that he was having the baby with was a bad element—she was raised in foster care, her mother was a heroin addict and she had been surrounded by criminals. He was out of his depth because he'd never been raised like that, but the drugs had taken him and he was at rock bottom. He had heroin, alcohol and benzodiazepines—everything—on board.

My grandson was born a few months later, and throughout the rest of the pregnancy I had to hang in there and deal with this woman because, if this was Kane's child, I had to make sure he was going to be okay.

Kane died in December, the baby was born in May, and DOCs removed him after three weeks because he was born full of amphetamines. Then they rang me and asked if I still wanted to care for the baby and I've had him ever since. He's five now.

The Mirabel Foundation (a Melbourne-based organisation supporting children orphaned by parental drug abuse—www.mirabelfoundation.com) was very kind to me during my darkest days. I spent a lot of hours crying on the phone to them. They are always sending me money to pay for his swimming lessons and things like that. It helps when you are raising a child again.

There have been times when I have been so exhausted and have hit the wall, but in terms of loving my grandson and looking at him and knowing that he is my son's child, it is mixed emotions. It is hard.

Through FDS I now realise that there are a lot of people going through what I was going through.

At the time, I didn't know that, because when it's happening you tend not to talk about it. I didn't have anyone to talk to because I really thought I was alone.

The advice from FDS actually relieves you of guilt, because you don't want to kick your child out but you need to feel supported in what you feel you have to do to care for them.

I feel really passionate about FDS, even though it's not for me now. It's not about grief, FDS, it's about helping the living. It's about keeping people alive long enough until they can seek help or put their hand up for help. It's about helping you stay strong so that you can help your loved one who's drug-dependent. I feel really cheated that I never found FDS while Kane was alive. With all the professionals that I dealt with during Kane's ten-year journey—doctors, police, paramedics, hospital staff, counsellors—nobody ever turned to me and said, 'How are you coping?' Nobody ever asked how my marriage was holding up, or how I was doing after sitting by my son's bedside all night after he'd overdosed. That's where FDS helps people. If you can get that help—if you can cope—then there's more chance that your loved one will be okay.

The reality of having a child addicted to drugs is very, very hard.

These stories are from just two of the hundreds of families in Australia who have paid the ultimate price for drug use. Every year we hold remembrance ceremonies for the families of those who have died. The ceremony was first started in Canberra, by Marion and Brian McConnell, who lost their son to overdose. They run an organisation called 'Families and Friends for Drug Law Reform', and FDS collaborates with them on many projects. Brian and Marion are also long-term volunteers on the FDS Helpline.

The ceremonies are held in the third weekend of October, in several Australian locations and, although sad, are also healing events that give grieving families the opportunity to acknowledge that their loved ones were important parts of their lives—people who had personalities, talents and qualities that made them so much more than just drug users.

As a grieving parent myself, I have learned that, although my relationship with Damien has changed forever, I do continue to have a relationship with him. I talk to him, occasionally, in my mind. I remember him regularly and with much love, but now, more than a decade on, there are often times that he may not come to mind for a few days. I still dream about him sometimes—but not as often as I once did. Myself, my wife Sandra, and my other children still 'include' him in family activities and honour his memory by lighting a large candle on important occasions such as Christmas, birthdays and the anniversary of his death.

Losing a child is the hardest bereavement. I have lost all my grandparents, both of my parents, my brother and many friends and acquaintances, but none of those losses—although painful—was like the feeling that overwhelms you when your child dies. Children are not meant to die before their parents. It is not natural. The fact that the death has been brought about by the use of drugs brings even more burdens. Why? Because there is always that haunting knowledge that—unlike terminal illness or random accident—the death was preventable. Nobody needs to die from a drug overdose.

The other reason that the loss of a child to drugs is so difficult is that, in the eyes of many in the community, including police, people of the church and even some family and acquaintances, our loved ones who have died are seen as criminals or sinners. The weight of this enforced shame can cause bereaved families to suffer through their loss in silence—some even inventing other reasons to publicly explain the cause of death.

Bereavement should not be so masked. Talk to friends, or seek professional counselling if it helps, and remember—your healing will not diminish the memory of your loved one.

Even though I no longer wallow in my grief for Damien, his presence will never be far from my heart and mind, and I know that he will not truly die until his siblings, his family members and all those who knew and loved him and carry the memory of him eventually die. Grief does not need to overtake the rest of your living years. You may feel guilt that you are here and your loved one is not, but that feeling will not bring them back, and will only make you, and those also still living in your life, unhappy and unfulfilled. Many people become volunteers on the FDS helpline to make some sense out of what often seems senseless.

Don't forget the past but do look to the future. It can, and will, get better if you let it.

CHAPTER 11

Life Must Go On

Since Damien died, a lot of things have happened. One of the tragic things is that, during these last ten years, we have lost probably 6000 or 7000 people to illicit drugs, and probably another 50000 to alcohol-related causes. That is a national disgrace and a national tragedy. The dead were someone's son or daughter, brother or sister, father or mother. Despite the pain of these confronting statistics, there are some positives. Perhaps even with overwhelming tragedy comes some form of healing.

I do think that even though there is still room for improvement, families who are affected by problems of drug and alcohol dependency are getting a better look-in and are now more acknowledged and understood. I believe that we at Family Drug Support have had some small part in making that happen, and for that I am very, very proud.

On a personal level, I have had the opportunity to travel to some parts of Australia that I had never seen before, and have also travelled around the world, speaking at conferences and meeting so many amazing family members who are living through this difficult experience.

I have, too, received accolades and awards—including, in 2008, the Prime Minister's Award for Alcohol and Drug Treatment Excellence—things I view as a great personal honour, but also as definite proof that the work of Family Drug Support is being recognised and appreciated by people outside of the immediate impact of drug dependency. Some years ago I was given an international award at a conference in Melbourne, and in accepting that award I spoke about my travels and my previous accolades, and how much those opportunities had meant to me, but I also said that, quite honestly, I would give it all away for just ten minutes with my son. Throughout my time at the helm of FDS, I have never stopped thinking about why I do this and what motivates me, and I would like to think that Damien would be pretty proud of what FDS has achieved.

It is too late for Damien—too late for me as his father to ever have him in my life again—but I know that there are many, many people for whom it is not too late. Don't let it be too late. By looking at the strategies in this book as a starting point, you really can make a difference in your own life and the life of your drug user. And maybe, together, we can all make a difference to the futures of other Australians too.

In order to make this broader difference, we, as a nation, need to be more understanding—understanding of the physical and mental effects drugs can have, of course, but also understanding and supportive of the people who succumb to them.

Heroin trafficker Nguyen Tuong Van was executed in Singapore's Changi Prison in November 2005, after receiving a mandatory death sentence. He was caught, in 2002, at Changi Airport on his way home to Melbourne, carrying nearly fourteen ounces of heroin. Supporters of FDS played an active role in trying to get some action to change that decision.

A lot of people wonder why the families who have been affected by heroin would want to save the lives of any people who are convicted traffickers in heroin, but I guess I see the decisions made by the young people such as the Bali Nine or Nguyen as very similar to those of my own son. Damien made a stupid decision—probably without proper thought of the consequences—and threw my life, and the lives of so many people who loved him, into complete chaos. I see the families of the Bali Nine as being in exactly the same position as my family, and I think that view is shared by most of the members of FDS, who can also relate to the confusion and sadness that they have felt in dealing with their own drug user.

When we went out on a limb to support the Nguyen Tuong Van case, we received lots of messages of support from people all over Australia, and, amid all that, I think I only had one negative phone call. Even then, the woman who rang me to express her negativity later rang me back to say that she had changed her mind. That tells me that the people of this country, if not the government, are ready to move forward. Now we just need to convince our leaders to take action, make changes and, hopefully, save lives.

It is interesting to note that a lot of Asian countries that used to have a zero-tolerance approach are now moving to harm-reduction policies.

In terms of the way that the so called Bali Nine were initially arrested, I am very critical of the actions of the Australian Federal Police. I do not understand why these young people were arrested in Indonesia when our authorities could have waited until they were on the plane and coming back home to Australia. It has always appeared to be politically motivated and if we are to change anything to improve the lives of future generations of Australians, then the government's response to the drug issue should never be about political grandstanding, but rather about seeking out innovative policies that might really have a positive long-term effect. It is important that we don't take out our anger at the drug trade on the drug mules.

Back in the early days of FDS, heroin was, very visibly, a major problem that appeared to be always in the media. And as long as it was in the media, we always got attention. With those days gone, though, getting publicity—and the weight of any genuine political interest—for the problem that bubbles beneath the surface of just about every Australian neighbourhood, has been increasingly challenging. Every now and then you might see overblown news reports about whatever the drug du jour is—amphetamines, ice or cocaine—but, once the ratings period dies down, the problem is quickly forgotten again and there is still no solution.

Media in Australia do love to provoke polarisation, and politicians—especially conservative politicians—seem to love that too. I think one of the things that has always frustrated me is that politicians tend to have a very short-term view when it comes to dealing with drugs. They want something that makes an immediate impact and looks as though it has solved the problem—obviously better for the evening news sound-bite or splash of attention on the newspaper's front pages. Consequently, they tend to implement strategies that are very short-term and do almost nothing to really solve, or even alleviate, the long-term nature of the problem.

I think what we need to do as we look to the future is to be more strategic and more long-term in our thinking. We need to start being realistic and look on drugs as an issue that, really, we are never going to solve. Obviously, it would be great if we could, but the reality is that it won't happen. After all, we're talking about something that is one of the biggest industries in the world—something that many people across the globe benefit from financially. No matter what we do, the drugs seem to flourish.

We are living in a time when the spread of the Internet has ensured the widespread dissemination of information about how to actually manufacture drugs in home laboratories. It just means that there are more and more drugs coming onto the market. We must face the fact that we are not going to stop it—ever. What we need to do is to learn how to live with this and learn how to manage it as safely as possible—anything to ensure that our young people don't keep dying. As I wrote in Chapter 9, I think that we need to look at practical strategies of harm minimisation and decriminalisation as a possible answer.

At first glance, these thoughts could come across as 'giving up'—someone resigned to a problem too huge to fix. I am not giving up, though. Supporting the concept of harm minimisation and decriminalisation does not mean that I am surrendering, or losing a battle in what so many sensationalised media reports refer to as 'the war on drugs'. Implementing harm minimisation strategies that include safe injecting facilities, distribution of clean needles and honest information, as well as controlled doses of a substance that might otherwise be sourced in dirty alleyways from unscrupulous drug dealers, is something that I see as not only potentially life-saving but also extremely realistic and practical—things long missing from the highly emotional debate that tends to surround the issue of drug use.

Not all families agree with harm minimisation. Although

most of those who have dealt with the drug issue for a long time do accept it there have been high-profile cases where the policy has been criticised. I find this very sad. Simple harm-minimisation strategies can save people's lives including the children of some of the critics.

With Damien's death, I have witnessed first-hand the havoc and devastation that drugs can cause to families, and I certainly do not want to be seen as someone who is promoting drug use. I have never promoted it and certainly never will. I do not want to be part of anything that condones drug use. Harm minimisation is not about giving permission or approval. It is simply about saving lives.

If we handle this correctly, I do believe that things can and will change. Prohibition is not the answer. I think that we need to take a similar model to that which has been applied to nicotine. Lots of warning signs, no promotion of it—no positive marketing.

I think it is time to have a debate and, while I don't think that Australia is ready to go the whole hog yet, I do believe that we are ready to at least start the discussions—openly and honestly.

Human beings have always used some types of drugs—that's part of our condition. It's not going to go away. My vision for a happier, healthier future is that, eventually, we will find drugs that are safe—things that can replicate the feelings that drug users seek out, without the damage to so many lives. But then I am asked, if we really do learn to make drugs that don't cause any harm, what will the risk-takers do then? Something else, I guess—but let's worry about that if it happens.

At the time of writing we are launching a new initiative, 'Bridging the Divide', funded by the Commonwealth Government. It is a program to include family members in the treatment process and give them information and realistic expectations of this process. Our three new project officers will take this program across Australia.

For families still living with the traumatic impact of drugs and alcohol in their lives—life really does go on. I appreciate that this sounds simplistic and may be hard to believe . . . but it does.

You can't immediately change the behaviour of the drug user in your life—no matter how much you ache to—but you can change your own life and your attitude to the way that they are living theirs. With that change, all kinds of wonderful things can eventually transpire—with patience and perseverance and, if it works for you, perhaps even prayer. Life, no matter how many obstacles there are in your way, does go on. Keep living your life in the way that is best for you and the other loved ones who are part of it, and good luck.

appendix
Know Your Product

Liz, 60, first became aware that her son had a problem with alcohol when he was 24. The problem extended to cannabis and speed. He is now 32 and Liz believes that things are getting better.

Knowledge takes away the fear of the unknown and you know what you're dealing with, rather than just worrying about something that is lurking in the background. That could be just learning about the drug they are using—what the effects are. It makes you more understanding of what they are going through and how they're feeling on a particular day.

By learning about drugs and their effects, family members and friends can better learn to help the drug user. This chapter outlines Australia's most commonly used and abused drugs, with descriptions of the drugs' effects, associated risks and typical behaviours, and also important information about treatment options. Knowledge is power. Remember, if you suspect an overdose, always call an ambulance on 000.

The information contained in this chapter is not recommended to be read by children. It is printed here as a resource for adults who want to gain knowledge that may help them cope with a drug user in their family. For further information or support see the list of national and state providers at the end of this book.

ALCOHOL

Alcohol is also known as booze, turps, grog, goon and piss.

History of the drug

Alcohol is the most commonly used drug in Australia, but is not always regarded as a 'drug'. While it is true that drinking in moderation does not harm most people, regular excessive drinking of alcohol is associated with a variety of health, personal and social problems. In 1992 the National Health and Medical Research Council developed a first set of guidelines for the Australian public to minimise harms associated with alcohol use. These have now been revised. Further information about them can be obtained from www.alcoholguidelines.gov.au.

A standard drink is any drink that contains 10 grams (or 12.5 millilitres) of alcohol. For low-risk drinking the following recommendations are made for men and women.

Women should drink no more than:

- 2 standard drinks a day and no more than 14 standard drinks in a week
- 4 standard drinks on any one occasion.

Women should have one or two alcohol-free days a week.

Men should drink no more than:

- 4 standard drinks a day and no more than 28 standard drinks in a week
- 6 standard drinks on any one occasion.

Men should have one or two alcohol-free days a week.

Medical research is still investigating if safe drinking levels exist for pregnant women. Until results are more conclusive, pregnant women or women intending to become pregnant are recommended to consider not drinking at all. They are advised not to become intoxicated. The first few weeks after conception are probably the most critical in relation to alcohol, but women may not be aware of the pregnancy at this stage. Alcohol use during pregnancy can harm the unborn baby. It has been linked with higher risk of miscarriage or stillbirth. The most serious outcome is foetal alcohol syndrome, which affects the infant both physically and mentally. Women who are breastfeeding are advised to also follow the same recommendations as pregnant women, as alcohol in the bloodstream passes into breast milk.

Forms of the drug

Alcohol is available in various strengths as a liquid. This is usually recorded on the bottle as a percentage by volume. Common types are wine, beer, ports/sherries and spirits, but people can also drink methylated spirits. Most alcohol products will label the number of standard drinks in each container. A standard drink contains 10 grams of alcohol.

Standard drinks for common drinks:

- For light beer this is equal to one schooner.
- For full-strength beer this is equal to one middy.
- For wine this is equal to one small glass, which is 100 mL.
- For fortified wines, such as port or sherry, a standard drink is one 60 mL glass.
- For spirits it is one nip, which is 30 mL.

The blood–alcohol concentration will generally remain below 0.05 if a man of average size drinks no more than two standard drinks in the first hour and one per hour thereafter and a woman of average size drinks no more than one standard drink per hour.

Effects

Alcohol is a depressant and slows down parts of the brain and the nervous system. Alcohol passes straight into the bloodstream from the small intestine and stomach.

Higher doses of alcohol can produce hallucinations, irrational behaviour, vomiting and convulsions. Alcohol can also trigger aggression. Anyone who regularly drinks a lot of alcohol will probably experience some physical, emotional or social problems.

Alcohol is broken down into other substances by the liver. A healthy liver takes about an hour to break down one standard drink. When sobering up it takes time for the liver to do its job. Despite the myths, black coffee, cold showers, exercise or vomiting do not speed up the work of the liver. Vomiting will remove only the alcohol in the stomach that has not had time to be absorbed into the bloodstream, therefore at most, only the last drink will be eliminated. Taking a shower or drinking black coffee may help someone to feel more awake, but it will not reduce the alcohol content in their blood.

Risks and harms

Because of the effects of alcohol on judgement and performance, blood–alcohol levels are stipulated for some occupations and for driving a motor vehicle. A blood–alcohol concentration (BAC) of up to 0.05 is allowed under most state laws for fully licensed drivers. Alcohol is implicated or involved in the majority of road accidents and domestic violence, and around 30 per cent of deaths by drowning are alcohol-related.

Alcohol is responsible for the majority of drug-related deaths in 15–34 year olds. Among Australian teenagers, 'binge drinking' (drinking to get drunk, e.g. more than five drinks in a row) is an increasing and worrying phenomenon. Risks associated with this include:

- internal physical damage including brain damage, overdose/unconsciousness
- higher risk of being involved in car accidents, fights or criminal behaviour
- an increased risk of sexual assault for females
- an increase in risk-taking behaviour such as using other drugs, having unsafe sex, climbing bridges, diving off jetties, or swimming at night
- domestic violence
- fights and other physical assaults.

Combining alcohol with any other drug is extremely dangerous. Loss of control and judgement can lead to intoxication and/or risky use of other drugs including unsafe injection practices or experimentation. Mixing alcohol with tranquillisers or sedatives can significantly increase the risk of overdose. A majority of fatal heroin overdoses have alcohol in their blood as well. Combining alcohol with over-the-counter or prescribed medications may decrease their effectiveness and will increase the side effects of both.

Dependency

People who regularly drink can develop tolerance and will need to drink larger amounts of alcohol to get the same effects as before. Regular drinkers can also become dependent on alcohol. Alcohol-free days are therefore recommended to assist people to remain in control of their drinking and within the recommended guidelines.

Overdose

Alcohol is a central nervous system depressant, and drinking too much can cause the body and nervous system to shut down to the point of unconsciousness and, in severe cases, coma, with accompanying risk of brain damage or death.

Withdrawal

Withdrawal/detox from alcohol is extremely stressful—both physically and mentally—and carries higher physical risks than withdrawal from many other drugs: for example, shakes, hallucinations or fitting. People should *never* give up alcohol 'cold turkey'.

Detox and treatment

Whether being done at home or at a detox centre, detox from alcohol should be closely supervised. Withdrawal takes several weeks, and psychological dependency continues for some time (or forever) after physical detox.

There are medical and non-medical, private and public detox centres available for alcohol withdrawal. Phone your state's Alcohol and Drugs Info Service for details of services providing alcohol detox and support programs.

Different treatments and approaches will suit different people, and more than one option may have to be tried. Treatment and rehabilitation ranges from the twelve-step abstinence-based model to controlled drinking programs being offered at many outpatient counselling centres. Naltrexone (also used for heroin withdrawal) has been used in the treatment of alcohol dependency, most positively for the prevention of relapse.

When to call an ambulance

If they have been drinking and pass out, or become unable

to speak or move, then call 000. If they are still breathing and have a pulse, lie them on their side in the safety position while waiting for the ambulance. This is because unconscious people have a high risk of vomiting and choking to death. Make sure their airways are clear, and ensure that they are not left alone.

If they have no pulse and are not breathing, commence CPR (Cardiopulmonary Resuscitation) immediately. If they have a pulse but are NOT BREATHING, commence mouth-to-mouth resuscitation ONLY.

AMPHETAMINES

Currently, in Australia, amphetamines come in many different forms and users refer to them by many different names, including speed, go-ee, whiz, uppers, dexies, buzz, rev, crystal, crystal meth, base, pure, ice, shabu and ox blood.

History of the drug

Amphetamines were developed in the United States during the 1920s. By the 1960s, doctors in Australia were prescribing them as a decongestant and to treat obesity and depression. During World War II and the Korean and Vietnam wars, soldiers on all sides of the conflicts were given amphetamines to keep them awake, to give them more energy and to suppress their appetites.

Forms of the drug

The term 'amphetamine' refers to a whole family of synthetic drugs that are all chemically related to amphetamine and have pretty similar effects. The amphetamine family of drugs falls into the class of drugs known as stimulants. Speed is manufactured illegally and is available as a powder that can vary in texture from very fine to more coarse and crystalline, and can also vary in colour from white to yellow, pink or brownish. It is occasionally found in liquid form. All these variations occur because the purifying process involved in the manufacture of amphetamine is quite involved and most of the people who make the drug don't have the chemical expertise to do it properly. This means that, although they're all making speed, they end up with a wide range of products at the end of the manufacturing process, which look different and contain different levels of impurities. 'Base' is an oily powder. 'Ice' and 'shabu' are strong and more potent forms of amphetamine that come in the form of a crystal, rather than a powder. 'Ox blood' is a liquid form of speed.

No matter what form it comes in, almost all of the speed available in Australia today is methamphetamine. Methamphetamine is slightly different in chemical terms to amphetamine but the two have very similar effects. Although the availability and use of crystalline forms of methamphetamine are increasing, most of the speed available in Australia these days still comes in the form of powder.

Speed may be swallowed, snorted or injected. Some of the people who use the crystalline forms known as 'ice' or 'shabu' smoke it in a special glass pipe. Injecting and smoking are the more harmful ways to use speed. Injecting is the most dangerous method of use, as tolerance (resistance) develops quickly and leaves the user needing higher quantities of the drug in order to achieve the same 'rush'. Smoking is also an efficient means of getting it into the system.

Tablets with chemical compositions similar to amphet-amines such as dexamphetamine, Duromine and Ritalin, which are prescribed for Attention Deficit Hyperactivity Disorder (ADHD) or for narcolepsy (a condition of constant sleepiness), are occasionally used by speed users for their stimulant properties.

Effects

Amphetamines are stimulants and increase the activity of the central nervous system and produce effects similar to the body's naturally occurring 'fight or flight' hormone, adrenalin. The actual effect will depend on the form and type of drug, its purity (as illegal drugs may often be mixed with other substances), as well as the amount taken, and also whether other drugs, caffeine drinks or alcohol have been consumed as well. The person's expectations and experience with the drug, combined with the mood and environment they are in, will also have an influence on effects.

Speed makes people feel uninhibited. Using speed with alcohol severely increases the risks of unsafe driving, sex, or other drug use—with the accompanying risks of death, infection and injury.

Injecting speed users are at risk of transmission of infectious diseases such as Hepatitis C and HIV (AIDS). Speed users do not usually know exactly what is in the drug they are taking. Amphetamines are rapidly absorbed from oral consumption and reach a peak concentration in two hours, with the effect of a single dose lasting 5–20 hours. When amphetamines are injected the effect is rapid and wears off quickly.

Short-term effects of amphetamine use may include:

- euphoria and wellbeing
- increased energy and hyperactivity
- talkativeness
- reduction of appetite ·
- dry mouth
- increased blood pressure and heart rate
- nausea.

Long-term effects of amphetamine use may include:

- sleep problems
- extreme mood swings
- compulsive repetition of actions
- paranoia
- depression and anxiety
- panic attacks
- seizures
- social and financial problems.

Risks and harms

One of the greatest problems experienced by amphetamine users is amphetamine-induced psychosis, or 'speed psychosis'. The symptoms of speed psychosis are similar to those of paranoid schizophrenia, and may include hallucinations, paranoid delusions, or uncontrolled violent behaviour. This state usually disappears after the drug has been eliminated from the body, although the user remains vulnerable to further episodes in the future. If the drug is used again, the psychosis may recur.

Dependency

Regular users can develop a tolerance to speed and will need greater quantities to get the same effects as before. Some people can also become dependent on speed. They have a strong desire to continue its use, and if speed is unavailable they may panic or become anxious. Users may take speed continually over a long period followed by a period of exhaustion and crashing, during which time sedatives such as benzos (see page 174) or heroin may be taken to aid the 'coming down' process.

Overdose

The risk of amphetamine overdose is low but can cause brain

haemorrhage, heart attack, high fever or coma. Deaths may occur if the overdose is not medically treated.

Withdrawal

When a dependent person stops using speed or severely cuts down the amount they use they may experience symptoms such as:

- fatigue
- hunger
- deep depression
- disturbed sleep
- irritability
- agitation and anxiety.

Detox and treatment

Both private and public medical and non-medical detox centres are available for amphetamine withdrawal. Detox takes 3–5 days and is characterised by the symptoms listed above.

With professional support, supervised home detox is possible. Make sure a medical practitioner or drug and alcohol professional is available at all hours for information and support. Dial 000 if anything goes wrong or you feel you can't cope. Remember—detoxification is not a cure for dependency. Users have come to rely on speed for enjoying themselves and feeling good, and commonly feel unable to participate in social activities without using speed. Ongoing treatment, support and counselling may be necessary to resolve the psychological dependency and promote abstinence.

Commonly, paranoia and anxiety symptoms occur as part of amphetamine withdrawal and may make the withdrawing user aggressive and irrational. Do not put yourself or your family at risk—especially if you feel threatened by violent behaviour.

When to call an ambulance

Dial 000 immediately if someone:

- has heart palpitations, shortness of breath, wheezing, convulsions, severe headache, blurred vision, or collapses into unconsciousness following the use of speed
- passes out or becomes unable to speak or move, but is still breathing and has a pulse. Move them so they are lying on their side
- stops breathing. If a pulse cannot be felt, commence mouth-to-mouth resuscitation. If a pulse is felt DO NOT attempt CPR.

BENZODIAZEPINES

Benzodiazepines is the name of the group of drugs commonly known as benzos, minor tranquillisers, pills or sleepers.

Each drug has a chemical 'generic' name and at least one 'brand name'. Brand names are the same drug made by different companies. Some of the more common brand names are:

- Diazepam (Antenax, Ducene, Valium)
- Oxazepam (Alepam, Murelax, Serepax)
- Nitrazepam (Alodorm, Mogodon)
- Clonazepam (Rivotril)
- Tamazepan
- Flunitrazepam (Hypnodorm, Rohypnol—now unavailable).

The generic name is always printed on the manufacturer's label.

History of the drug

Benzodiazepines are restricted substances under the NSW *Poisons Act*. Illegal use, possession or supply carries a heavy fine or imprisonment. Many doctors treat anxiety and sleep problems by prescribing benzodiazepines. They can also be used to treat panic disorders and muscle spasms, and are occasionally used in the treatment of epilepsy. Benzodiazepines only treat the symptoms of these disorders, not the cause.

Under strict medical supervision, they may also be used to assist in alcohol withdrawal. Heroin, speed and ecstasy drug users tend to use benzos to help them sleep or when they are trying to withdraw or quit taking their drug. It is useful to know the generic name of these drugs, as some people will say they have stopped taking the drug when they have merely swapped to a different brand. Some people use benzos as their 'drug of choice'.

Forms of the drug

Benzodiazepines come in tablet form and should be taken orally. Some users crush and inject benzos, which is highly problematic and potentially dangerous. Some benzos are toxic to veins once injected.

Effects

Benzodiazepines affect the central nervous system. Like alcohol and heroin, they are depressants and slow down responses such as respiration, heart rate and mental and emotional responses. Subsequent dizziness, drowsiness and confusion are the cause of many accidents. Driving, operating machinery, or sometimes carrying out simple household chores such as cooking can be dangerous if a person is affected by benzos.

According to a study conducted by the National Drug and Alcohol Research Centre, almost half the benzo users surveyed reported having committed some form of property crime while under the influence of these pills.

Risks and harms

If a person is depressed, or has a family history of depression, the use of benzos carries a high risk of triggering a depressive episode, and are also used as a common method of suicide. Used together, alcohol and benzos are an extremely dangerous combination as the depressant effect of each is magnified. For those already feeling down or experiencing life problems, this combination intensifies and magnifies negative feelings and thoughts, increasing the risk of suicide or self-harming behaviour.

Dependency

Regular use of benzodiazepines is highly likely to produce physical and psychological dependence within about 4–6 weeks. For this reason, doctors should only usually prescribe them for very short periods of time, and monitor their use closely. Tolerance (resistance) increases quickly. After just three nights of taking sleeping tablets, users may quickly find themselves 'needing' to take larger doses to feel the same effect.

Overdose

Heroin and benzodiazepines can be a lethal combination. One in every four heroin-related deaths has involved combined use of these drugs. With benzos in a person's system, less heroin is needed to overdose. Even the day after a binge on benzos, which can then remain in the system for up to 24 hours, the risks of heroin use increase dramatically.

Overdose with benzodiazepines is quite possible and symptoms are similar to heroin overdose. Overdose risk is severely increased when benzos are combined with heroin or alcohol. Although it is common to hear that walking a person around, putting them under a shower, making them vomit, or even giving them tea or coffee, will reverse an overdose or 'bring them around', these are merely myths—and could all be very dangerous. Don't waste precious time that should be used calling an ambulance.

Withdrawal

Withdrawal from benzodiazepines can be dangerous, and should never be attempted suddenly. If possible, withdrawal from benzodiazepines should begin when there is some degree of stability in a person's life. Serious complications, such as fits or hallucinations, may occur if a person has been using benzos for more than 2–3 weeks. Users need to gradually reduce their dose under the supervision of a doctor, pharmacist or health worker.

Withdrawal symptoms can include:

- sleeping problems
- tension, muscle pain, pain attacks
- depression, sensory disturbances, fits, hallucinations
- sweating, anxiety and tremors.

Detox and treatment

Benzodiazepines are extremely difficult drugs to withdraw from and to stay away from. It takes many people several attempts before they are successful. Each attempt should be looked upon as part of the learning process, and users should be reminded that it is possible to try again.

Trying to work out what triggers the desire to use the benzodiazepines in the first place and developing alternative coping ideas and strategies can help. Keeping a diary may be useful to help identify triggers. Learning new ways to cope with stress, insomnia and anxiety with the support of a drug counsellor, psychologist or supportive rehab centre can be extremely helpful during treatment and afterwards.

When to call an ambulance

- If you are unable to wake someone up. A common myth is that a person is 'sleeping it off'. THIS IS NOT TRUE. If they don't respond to shaking and calling their name then they are in danger of dying or being seriously injured. Even snoring can be a sign of overdose.
- If you hear gurgling or choking sounds as they are breathing.
- If they have cold, clammy skin or are sweating profusely.
- If their eyes are open, but they are like 'doll's eyes'—staring or vacant.
- If they have passed out or become unable to speak or move. If they are still breathing and have a pulse, lie them on their side while waiting for the ambulance.
- If there is no pulse and they are not breathing: commence CPR immediately and wait for the ambulance. If there is a pulse but NO BREATHING, commence mouth-to-mouth resuscitation ONLY.

CANNABIS

Cannabis is the short name for the hemp plant Cannabis Sativa, also known as marijuana. Street or slang names include: pot, grass, dope, mull, yundi, hooch, dagga and hash.

History of the drug

The first known mention of cannabis was in a Chinese medical text of 2737BC. It has been used for many thousands of years to make products such as clothing and rope, and for medicinal and spiritual purposes. Despite this long history, it remains one of the least understood illicit drugs.

Cannabis is the most commonly used illicit drug in Australia and comes from the dried flowers and leaves of the cannabis plant. According to the 2004 National Drug Strategy Household Survey, more than one-quarter (26 per cent) of teenagers (persons aged 14–19) had used marijuana/cannabis in their lifetime. Across all age groups, males were more likely than females to have ever used cannabis, with the exception of 14–19-year-old females (26 per cent female/25 per cent male).

Australians aged 20–39 were more likely than those in the other age groups to have used cannabis at some time in their lives. Almost three in five (55 per cent) of persons aged 20–39 years had used cannabis in their lifetime.

Although once regarded as the 'safest' of the illegal drugs available, chronic use of cannabis is now associated with the development of psychological dependence, and recent research, combined with anecdotal evidence from many long-term users, indicates that physical and psychological dependence is possible with prolonged, heavy use, but is not inevitable.

The problems associated with cannabis these days are related to how it is used. In the past, the whole plant, including the less potent leaf, was smoked in hand-rolled cigarettes (joints), and usually only occasionally. Today, cannabis users tend to discard the leaf and take the more potent parts of the plant—buds and heads—which are then compressed and packed tightly into 'cones' and inhaled through 'bongs' or 'pipes'. As it is a much more efficient method of ingestion, the effects are far more intense. Users also tend to use more frequently, which then increases the risk of dependence.

Small amounts of cannabis do not appear to produce lasting harmful effects, and withdrawal is minimal or non-existent from all but heavy continuous use.

Forms of the drug

Cannabis leaf is usually smoked in water pipes called bongs or in hand-rolled cigarettes called joints. Hashish, or hash, is the resin of the plant. It is sold as oil or in compressed small blocks and is usually mixed with tobacco and smoked.

The chemical Delta–9 tetrahydrocannabinol, or THC, is what makes the user 'high'. The more THC cannabis contains, the stronger it is. The concentration of THC is higher and more potent in hash than in the leaf and flower heads of the plant. Cannabis leaf and hashish can also be cooked in foods such as 'hash cookies'.

Effects

The effects of cannabis depend on the amount taken, the person's experience with the drug, their expectations, the mood they are in, and the way in which the drug is taken. The effects of cannabis are most intense during the first hour after taking the drug, although they may persist for 3–5 hours.

Higher doses make these effects stronger. A person's perception of time, sound and colour may become distorted or sharpened. Feelings of excitement, anxiety or paranoia and confusion may also increase. Unlike alcohol and most other illicit drugs, THC does not act on the dopamine (pleasure) centres in the brain. The THC receptors are elsewhere in the brain and the immune system. Their purpose is not yet certain and the chemical effect of THC is not yet fully understood.

Frequent or heavy smokers commonly report some long-term effects, which recent research supports. Psychological effects include:

- decreased motivation, ambition and apathy
- reduced memory and learning abilities
- decreased sex drive and deterioration of social and communication skills
- impaired balance, coordination, logic, judgement, and concentration.

Risks and harms

The biggest risk with cannabis is of having accidents while driving, operating machinery, or at home. Once the person stops or reduces their use of cannabis these risks decline.

Long-term cannabis use also carries the same established risks as tobacco smoking, e.g. developing chronic respiratory problems, or lung, mouth or throat cancer from the carcinogens in the smoke. It is not wise to use any drugs during pregnancy. There is some evidence that cannabis used as an alternative to tobacco can contribute to lower birth weight and slower development in some babies.

Dependency

Regular users may develop a psychological dependence. This means they 'need' cannabis because it has become important in their daily lives—usually to relax, unwind, counter stress, or simply to make them feel at ease in social situations. Some research indicates that some heavy users of cannabis may develop physical dependency, as well as a higher tolerance (resistance), which means that with every subsequent usage, they need to use greater quantities of cannabis to get the same effects as before.

Extreme reactions are rare, although there is clinical recognition of cannabis users becoming disoriented, or suffering hallucinations or behavioural disturbances. Some researchers think cannabis use triggers episodes of pre-existing bipolar disorder (manic depression) or psychosis. It has also been shown by research to be linked to the development of schizophrenia in susceptible people. People suffering from depression are also likely to have a bad reaction to cannabis, and recent research indicates that the use of cannabis can precipitate depression in some vulnerable adolescents. Those people with a family history of mental illness should avoid cannabis or any other drug. Even people with less severe conditions like Asperger's syndrome can experience negative reactions when using cannabis.

Overdose

An overdose of cannabis is very unusual, but ingesting huge amounts has been known to cause people to fall into a coma and can make some users feel nauseous, paranoid, panicky and generally unwell.

Withdrawal

Withdrawal occurs when a heavy user stops using cannabis or severely cuts down the amount used. During withdrawal the person may experience:

- sleeping problems
- anxiety
- sweating
- loss of appetite, and an upset stomach.

These symptoms usually disappear within a few days, although sleep disturbance may last longer. Psychological attachments are similar to nicotine.

Detox and treatment

Treatment centres for cannabis-dependency are difficult to find, as acknowledging the possibility of physical dependency has only recently occurred. Home detox or withdrawal is a good option.

Treatment for psychological dependency on cannabis involves therapy or counselling to help the user understand why they use cannabis and how they can function without it. The National Drug and Alcohol Research Centre (NDARC) is currently carrying out research into cognitive behavioural interventions in cannabis use with very encouraging results, which will also have implications for treatments for other drugs.

Cognitive Behavioural Therapy (CBT) assists people to examine the behaviour and thought processes underlying heavy cannabis use, and helps them to develop skills to counteract the desire and craving to use cannabis.

There is now a new service—the National Cannabis Prevention and Information Centre (NCPIC)—and their helpline can be contacted on 1800 304050.

COCAINE

Cocaine is a drug derived from the leaves of the coca plant. Slang or street names include coke, blow, snow, Charlie, flake, stardust and crack. Crack is very rarely found in Australia.

History of the drug

Cocaine is a naturally occurring alkaloid found in the leaves of the coca bush. The leaves have been chewed by South American natives for hundreds of years in religious ceremonies and for their stimulant properties. After Columbus, they found their way to Europe and were used medicinally and as an anaesthetic for the eye until about 1950. It was part of the original formula for Coca-Cola and appeared in numerous patent medicines until it was banned from use in 1914.

Forms of the drug

Cocaine comes in the form of a white powder (cocaine hydrochloride) which can be snorted, injected, ingested, or converted to a free-base form and smoked. Smoking free-base cocaine, commonly known as crack, results in a quicker experience of the drug's pleasant effects. Crack is more concentrated than soluble cocaine. Most street cocaine is heavily 'cut' with various additives. Pure cocaine is rarely found on the street.

Effects

Cocaine is a central nervous system stimulant. Cocaine acts on the brain's pleasure and reward system and floods the brain with the naturally occurring neurotransmitter dopamine. Dopamine is normally associated with pleasurable feelings such as having sex, or satisfying hunger or thirst.

The brain quickly associates the memory of taking cocaine with the stimulation of its pleasure centres, and even recreational users can find themselves smelling cocaine for no reason, or experiencing a rush if they see a rolled-up bank note. Heavy cocaine users commonly report the desire to keep using continuously.

Short-term effects can occur rapidly after just a single dose ('line') of cocaine and can last anywhere from a few minutes to a few hours. Short-term cocaine use can also bring on aggressive behaviour and an inability to judge risks. The effects of cocaine tend to wear off quickly so people often take a number of small doses in quick succession. At higher doses, cocaine can produce headaches, dizziness, restlessness and violent behaviour. Other effects may include loss of concentration, a lack of motivation, heart pain and even heart attack.

Risks and harms

If cocaine is snorted, nose-bleeds are common, and damage to blood vessels may lead to holes in the supporting tissue of the nose. Injecting users also face the risk of contracting infectious diseases, such as Hepatitis C and HIV (AIDS).

When cocaine and alcohol are taken together, the two drugs combine to produce cocaethylene in the bloodstream. This chemical often creates the urge for more cocaine after a few drinks. This substance creates more damage to the brain than taking alcohol or cocaine individually.

Long-term use of cocaine can produce behavioural problems and psychosis.

Dependency

Cocaine is known to be extremely psychologically addictive. Laboratory animals that have been trained to press a lever to deliver an injection of cocaine will do so up to 300 times to receive a single dose. If given an unlimited supply they will continue to dose themselves until they die of exhaustion or a heart seizure. The pleasurable brain effects and feelings of increased confidence in oneself and one's abilities are thought to contribute greatly to the addictive nature of cocaine.

Overdose

The signs and symptoms of cocaine overdose are related to the psychological and stimulant effects of the drug. Classic signs of overdose are high blood pressure (hypertension) with a fast pulse (tachycardia) and an increased rate of breathing (tachypnea). This occurs with feelings of agitation, confusion, irritability, as well as sweating and hyperthermia (increased temperature). Sometimes, seizures may occur.

Cocaine overdose can also present as a heart attack with chest pain. This is thought to result from 'spasm' of the coronary arteries that feed the heart muscle, or from insufficient supply of blood flow to meet the needs of the stimulated heart muscle. In some cases, sudden death may also be the initial presentation to the emergency room. This is due to a lethal heart rhythm precipitated by cocaine consumption. Stroke, seizures, fever, infection, kidney failure, liver hepatitis, pneumonia, thrombophlebitis (clotting of the veins) and HIV are other potential complications of cocaine use and cocaine overdose.

Withdrawal

The withdrawal is known as 'cocaine dysphoria', or 'come-down', or 'crash'. Symptoms include:

- irritability
- extremes of hunger
- deep depression and suicidal feelings
- nausea and vomiting
- fatigue, weakness and muscle pain.

Detox and treatment

Home detox from cocaine is possible with the assistance of medical supervision and a support worker. Cocaine with-drawal symptoms can be difficult to manage as reactions can be unpredictable and sudden. You will need to keep a close watch for depression and suicidal thoughts, which could lead to a suicide attempt. If you are worried for any reason dial 000 for an ambulance immediately.

If the user has a history of mental illness, heart disease,

fits, high blood pressure or angina, detox would be safer in a clinical setting.

After detox, psychological dependency is common, and is regarded as the most severe of any illicit drug. Ongoing treatment and counselling will probably be needed to help with this.

When to call an ambulance

Dial 000 immediately if a person has heart palpitations, shortness of breath, wheezing, convulsions, severe headache, blurred vision, or collapses into unconsciousness after taking cocaine; or if they have passed out or become unable to speak or move. If they are still breathing and have a pulse—lie them on their side while waiting for the ambulance.

If there is no pulse and the person is not breathing, commence CPR and wait for the ambulance. If there is a pulse but NO BREATHING, commence mouth-to-mouth resuscitation ONLY.

The risk of overdose is severely increased when cocaine is combined with other drugs or alcohol. Death arising from first-time cocaine use is rare but possible, as some people have a severe reaction to even small doses.

ECSTASY AND OTHER PARTY DRUGS

Ecstasy is the common name for Methylenedioxy Meth-amphetamine, or MDMA. Street or slang names include ecky and E.

History of the drug

Ecstasy is known as the 'party' or 'love drug' and commonly makes users feel warm and loving, even towards people they may not know well. Ecstasy is a central nervous system stimulant primarily used as a party drug, in social situations. Its euphoric, mood-altering effects make it a popular stimulant for dancing and conversation.

Forms of the drug

Ecstasy is a synthetic drug usually sold as small tablets in a variety of colours and sizes. It also comes in capsule form, or as powder, and can be snorted or injected. Injecting ecstasy is becoming increasingly common, and is particularly risky because of the possible impurities present and the unpredictable composition of the tabs or capsules. Injecting users also face the risk of contracting infectious diseases such as Hepatitis C and HIV (AIDS).

Much of the so-called 'ecstasy' sold in Australia is in fact amphetamine.

Other party drugs

Other party drugs are Ketamine (Special K) and PCP (Angel Dust). These are anaesthetics with hallucinogenic effects. Apart from adverse reactions similar to those described for ecstasy, the main concern with Special K is the risk of being injured—due to its ability to block out pain. Ketamine is sometimes sold as ecstasy or mixed with ecstasy.

GHB (also known as GBH, Fantasy, Liquid E, G or Liquid X) is also an anaesthetic.

Effects

Ecstasy's effects depend on the amount taken, the person's experience with the drug, their expectations, the mood they are in and the way in which the drug is taken. Effects also depend on the quality and purity of the drug. Effects typically start within an hour of using the drug and can last up to six hours, but in some cases may last as long as 32 hours.

MDMA seems to work by boosting the levels of two brain chemicals:

- **serotonin**, which is the neurotransmitter that creates feelings of wellbeing and pleasure; and
- **dopamine**, which affects mood and muscle control, and also acts as a pain-suppressant.

Higher doses of ecstasy can produce hallucinations, irrational behaviour, vomiting and convulsions.

At low doses GHB induces a feeling of calm, relaxation and mild euphoria. At high doses it can cause sedation, nausea, vomiting, muscle stiffness, confusion, convulsions and, in some cases, coma or respiratory collapse. A number of fatalities in the US have been attributed to GHB.

Risks and harms

Other drugs are often used in combination with ecstasy as a way of coping with some of its undesirable effects. Little is known about the effects of these combinations but, in general, health risks tend to increase when any two or more drugs are used together, particularly if the doses are large.

Because serotonin and dopamine play a part in regulating body temperature, MDMA users may ignore the fact their body is overheating—simply because any messages of discomfort are prevented from being transmitted. High numbers of heat-related casualties and fatalities associated with the use of ecstasy are due to this effect. It appears to be the most common, immediate risk, so far, that is associated with ecstasy use.

It is important to keep sipping water while on ecstasy. Water does not dilute the effects of ecstasy—it only prevents dehydration. However, drinking too much water may lead to the brain swelling and irreversible damage in some people.

Dependency

Although it is still unclear whether physical dependence can develop, psychological dependence is a risk. People can develop tolerance (resistance) to the pleasurable effects of ecstasy, which means that, with subsequent usage, greater quantities of ecstasy are needed to get the same effects as before.

Those who become accustomed to partying and social-ising while on ecstasy may feel unable to communicate, make friends or enjoy themselves without using MDMA or a similar drug. Counselling and support may help with this dependency.

Extreme reactions to ecstasy are sporadic, impossible to predict, and appear unrelated to the amount taken. Reactions depend on a number of uncertain factors and relate to the individual's reaction at that particular time and place.

People who should never use MDMA or similar drugs include those with high blood pressure, a heart condition, diabetes, asthma, epilepsy, depression or other mental illness. Extreme reactions can include convulsions, mental disturbances, blood-clotting, liver damage and kidney failure, as well as hyperthermia—all of which can prove fatal. Some people appear to be more susceptible to the ill-effects of ecstasy.

Long-term risks are relatively unknown as yet, and research is continuing. Laboratory research with animals has pointed to the possibilities of long-term brain damage due to the destruction of brain cells that produce serotonin and, ultimately, failure of the brain to produce serotonin. Health professionals have also reported that some users continue to have psychiatric problems including delusions, depression, panic attacks, disorientation and depersonalisation. In a few cases, these symptoms have been permanent.

Overdose

Some of the main risks of ecstasy use are dehydration or heat stroke. Danger signs are sudden feelings of irritability, giddiness, cramps in the back of the legs, arms or back, passing little or dark-coloured urine, vomiting, or cessation of sweating. If these occur, sitting down in a cool, quiet place and sipping fluids such as fruit juice or water can help.

Be aware that drinking too much water may lead to brain swelling and irreversible damage in some people. If the symptoms continue, or worsen, seek immediate medical help.

When to call an ambulance

Call an ambulance immediately if a person has:

- heart palpitations, shortness of breath, wheezing, convulsions, severe headache, blurred vision, or collapses into unconsciousness following the use of ecstasy
- a severe headache and vomiting and they have injected ecstasy. This can indicate serious damage
- passed out or becomes unable to speak or move. If they are still breathing and have a pulse, lie them on their side while waiting for the ambulance
- no pulse and is not breathing. Commence CPR immediately
- a pulse but is NOT BREATHING. Commence mouth-to-mouth resuscitation ONLY.

HEROIN

Heroin belongs to the opioid drug group, and, like opium, morphine and codeine, comes from the opium poppy.

Pethidine and methadone are synthetically produced opioids. Street or slang names include smack, hammer, harry, dope, rocks, piss, shit and gear.

History of the drug

Heroin has been used for centuries for its pain-relieving properties.

Forms of the drug

Heroin can be injected, snorted or smoked by heating and inhaling the fumes (known as 'chasing the dragon'). It usually comes in powder form and can come in different colours.

Before being sold on the street, heroin is 'cut' or mixed with a cheap substance such as glucose, lactose or sucrose. It is rare (in Australia) for heroin to be cut with harmful contaminants.

Effects

The effects of heroin depend on the amount taken, the person's experience with the drug, their expectations, the mood they are in and the way in which the drug is taken. Effects also depend on the quality and purity of the drug. Heroin and other opioids are classified as central nervous system depressants. They act on the brain and nervous system by dulling perceptions of pain and fear, slowing breathing and reducing body temperature.

Heroin mimics the naturally occurring chemicals in the body which are produced in response to pain and which modify the effects of the pain-killing, pleasure-producing neurotransmitters called 'endorphins'. On entering the bloodstream, heroin releases a flood of endorphins. Physical effects include:

- a relaxed, 'cocooned' warm feeling and the disappearance of fear and worry following an initial rush of euphoria
- the skin becoming cold and the breath becoming slower and more shallow
- eyes glazing, and the user commonly appearing to be falling asleep where they sit or stand. This is known as being 'on the nod'.

At higher doses, the pupils of the eyes narrow to pin-points. This escape from reality to a warm, fuzzy world is perhaps the primary factor in continued heroin use and dependence, and the fear of returning to reality is a common barrier to cessation or reduction of use.

Adverse effects include nausea and vomiting, as well as constipation and itching. Constipation can continue for days or weeks, and can lead to hospitalisation and serious illness.

Risks and harms

Long-term heroin use may result in damage to the veins and the heart and lungs. Women may experience irregular menstruation and possibly infertility, while men may experience impotence. Sexual activity commonly becomes non-existent for regular heroin users, as the sexual drives fade, along with pain, fear and anxiety.

Because heroin is injected, users are at risk of contracting infectious diseases such as Hepatitis C or HIV (AIDS) through shared needles.

Street heroin is usually mixed with other substances such as glucose, which makes the strength of the drug difficult to determine. This can be a factor in accidental overdose.

Heroin can be dangerous when combined with other drugs, especially depressants such as alcohol, or minor tranquillisers such as Valium. These combinations can lead to coma or even death.

The use of heroin during pregnancy risks maternal and foetal health and may result in an underweight baby with retarded development. Methadone maintenance is strongly advised during pregnancy.

Dependency

Regular use of heroin is highly likely to produce dependence. Tolerance (resistance) to heroin increases rapidly, and the user quickly finds themselves chasing the experience of their first 'hit' with higher doses, while using regular 'maintenance' levels simply to 'get straight' or remove the unpleasant withdrawal effects.

Overdose

Too much heroin, morphine, methadone or opium causes the body to progress past contented drowsiness and into a state of coma. Overdose occurs as a result of the drug's effect on the central nervous system. The blood pressure drops so low that oxygen does not get to vital organs, the body shuts down, and breathing slows and stops.

Changes in the purity of heroin alone is rarely the cause of overdose. The majority of overdoses are accidental and occur when drugs are mixed. The first overdose usually happens after the person has been using for two years or more; and the majority of overdose-related fatalities occur when the person is alone.

Paramedics or medical staff treat an overdose by administering 'Narcan', which immediately reverses the effect of the heroin. It is a common myth that Narcan 'cleans' the system of heroin or methadone. The effects of Narcan are only temporary, and once it wears off it is possible to go back into overdose. Using again, straight after a Narcan-induced revival, could lead to another overdose. Similarly, if the user has taken other drugs when the Narcan is administered, these drugs will still affect them. Narcan only works for opioids.

Withdrawal

Withdrawal occurs when a dependent person stops using heroin or severely cuts down the amount used. Restlessness increases, followed by yawning, a runny nose, a craving for the drug, stomach cramps, diarrhoea, nausea, aching muscles, trembling, sweating and body spasms. These symptoms can be quite prolonged, but usually peak in 2–3 days.

Sudden withdrawal from heroin very rarely causes death unless the person has other medical complications or is withdrawing from another drug at the same time. Withdrawal from heroin can actually be less dangerous than withdrawal from alcohol or minor tranquillisers.

Detox and treatment

Methadone maintenance treatment, as well as treatment with other, newer pharmacotherapies, is useful in the treatment of opiate-dependence. It may take several attempts before the person is successful. Each attempt should be looked upon as a learning process: know that it is possible to try again.

Trying to work out what triggers the desire to use in the first place and developing coping ideas and strategies can help. Learning new ways to cope with insomnia with the support of a drug counsellor, psychologist, or supportive rehab centre can be extremely helpful during treatment and afterwards.

Detox can be accomplished rapidly with the use of naltrexone, or by giving up 'cold turkey' over a period of 5–7 days, and the symptoms can be relieved with medication— either as an in-patient or through home detox. As the person is at risk of reverting to heroin use, many people choose one of the pharmacotherapy treatments which include naltrexone or maintenance with methadone or buprenorphine.

Your support role during withdrawal in your home

It is useful to have an assessment to check if home detox is the best choice for you and to organise for a doctor or drug and alcohol worker to provide advice. Contact the intake worker at your local detox centre for information on how to arrange an assessment.

As a support person, it is important to be positive, calm and create a safe atmosphere in the home. You need to remember that you can be a powerful influence for change in your family. You know the person and will, with a bit of preparation, be able to help.

Spending time with the person—particularly during the first week of symptoms—may require you to re-organise your usual schedule. It can be good to have others with you who can give you some 'time out', as needed. Remember, you can phone the FDS line for help at any time, 24 hours, seven days.

You may have to take time off work and get some additional assistance for looking after other family members, such as younger children or elderly parents. You will need to decide how to explain to the drug user what is going to happen to them. You will also need to discourage drug-using friends of the drug user from visiting them during this time, and also keep people away who may cause stress or arguments. If your family member has an individual home detox support worker they will be able to assist you and answer any questions you may have either by phone or when they visit. If the person should convulse, experience chest pains, become unconscious, hallucinate or have other worrying symptoms, call an ambulance immediately.

You can help support by:

- understanding that detox does not mean a cure
- being willing to listen to the person
- helping the person to manage any physical pain and discomfort, e.g. cramps, vomiting or diarrhoea. If the nausea, vomiting and diarrhoea is severe then medication such as Maxalon or Lomotil may be helpful. The user's doctor can help by prescribing this. You can also use acupuncture pressure points to encourage their stomach to settle
- encouraging them to drink and eat small amounts of food. It is important to make sure the person doesn't get dehydrated, that they take lots of fluid (about 2 litres a day), and take light food such as soup, rice, noodles, vegetables, and fruit
- being patient
- trying not to argue with the person at this time
- encouraging the person to relax by reminding them of techniques they may know, e.g. controlled relaxed breathing, meditation, listening to tapes, music, relaxing in a shower or bath
- helping to distract and reassure the user through any cravings they may have, e.g. by doing an activity (watch a video, play cards, listen to music), delaying (suggest and encourage them to put off the decision for an hour) and drinking lots of water
- discussing and reminding them to look at their reasons for stopping
- doing some gentle exercise with them, e.g. walking, stretching, yoga or tai chi
- encouraging them to ease aches and pains by having warm baths or spas

- reminding them to contact other support people that are available in your area. (These contacts can help both you and your family member.)
- knowing what to do if an emergency situation occurs. (It is helpful if someone in the family understands some basic first aid skills.)
- avoiding in-depth counselling during detox as the person is vulnerable and having to cope with deep emotions may create more stress and not be helpful
- following any advice given to you by health workers to prevent the spread of infection.

When to call an ambulance

- If you are unable to wake someone. A common myth is that a person is 'sleeping it off'. THIS IS NOT TRUE. If they don't respond to shaking and calling their name, they are in danger. Be especially aware that snoring is a danger signal.
- If you hear gurgling or choking sounds as they are breathing.
- If they have cold, clammy skin or are sweating profusely.
- If their eyes are open, but they are like 'doll's eyes'—staring or vacant.
- If they have passed out or become unable to speak or move. If they are still breathing and have a pulse, lie them on their side while waiting for the ambulance.
- If there is no pulse and the person is not breathing. Commence CPR immediately and wait for the ambulance.
- If there is a pulse but NO BREATHING. Commence mouth-to-mouth resuscitation ONLY.

INHALANTS

Inhalant-sniffing is the common term for people becoming affected from breathing in the fumes from various solvents or gases. Inhalant use is also known as glue-sniffing, volatile-substance or solvent abuse. Products used for 'sniffing' include: glues, aerosols, liquid paper thinners, toluene, butane gas (lighter refills), nitrous oxide and petrol.

Forms of the drug

Glues and aerosol-can contents are commonly sprayed into a small plastic bag. The bag is then held over the mouth and nose and the contents inhaled. Others are inhaled directly from their containers, or soaked onto a piece of cloth. Sometimes, substances are sprayed directly into the nose or mouth—an extremely dangerous practice which can paralyse the airways, freeze the throat and cause suffocation.

Effects

Solvents are central nervous system depressants, like alcohol. However, because they are inhaled and go directly into the bloodstream, solvents act much more quickly than alcohol, with a greater potential for harm.

The initial effects, within 2–5 minutes of using, are feelings of excitement and relaxation. Repeated sniffing sustains these feelings. Loss of coordination also occurs. Some users become disoriented and frightened, and others experience side-effects such as blackouts and mild hallucinations.

Risks and harms

The dangers of inhalants depend on many different factors, including who is using and why, which substances are being inhaled, how and where. Some substances are less harmful than others.

The main danger of inhalants comes from accidents arising from being 'high' and losing inhibitions and judgement. Incidents such as falling, being run over, suffocation from plastic bags and reckless behaviour are common.

Short-term use of most products rarely leads to serious damage to the body. Some users have been admitted to hospital with convulsions, or because they are unable to control their movements or speak properly. Most of these symptoms clear within a few hours. Others experience problems with airways and breathing—however, this improves over time.

Long-term or heavy use of inhalants can lead to more damage as the substances build up in the body. Permanent damage to the brain, liver and kidneys has been reported in heavy, long-term users.

Practical advice for sniffers or potential sniffers includes such things as:

- do not sniff alone or in dangerous places
- do not put plastic bags over your head
- use small rather than large plastic bags to reduce the risk of suffocation
- do not smoke while sniffing as the substances used are highly flammable
- do not use other drugs while sniffing as this increases the risk of accidents.

Dependency

Only a very small number of young people try solvents, and for most of these the practice is experimental and social—done to fit in with a peer group or for 'kicks'. Part of the attraction is that solvents are a cheap and easy-to-obtain alternative to alcohol. Fortunately, in the majority of cases, this behaviour usually passes fairly quickly.

A small number of users do, however, go on to become 'long-term' or 'dependent' users of inhalants. Generally speaking, this category of high-risk users have other problems in their lives, and often have less familial support and little ability to deal with those problems. They may sniff alone or with other users, and are also likely to be using inhalants in combination with a variety of other drugs and alcohol.

Overdose

A rare occurrence with substances such as correcting fluids, butane gas and aerosol sprays is 'sudden sniffing death', where a user's heart can be caused to beat irregularly. These deaths are often associated with stress during or soon after sniffing, and, with that in mind, sniffers should never be chased or frightened.

Withdrawal

If a person who has been regularly using inhalants stops suddenly then acute withdrawal may be experienced. Symptoms may include:

- anxiety
- chills, shakes and tremors
- depression
- hallucinations
- stomach aches
- headaches
- loss of appetite
- nausea and dizziness
- imitation and aggressive behaviour

Detox and treatment

Seek medical advice or contact your local drug support service for information on detox and treatment for users of inhalants.

When to call an ambulance

If a person is drowsy or unconscious dial 000 for an ambulance, then lay them on their side to prevent choking if they vomit. Take away what they have been sniffing and, if the person is conscious, make sure they are breathing fresh air. Keep them calm and relaxed until they have completely sobered up, and don't chase them or get them stressed or panicked.

PSYCHEDELICS

Psychedelics are also known as hallucinogens. They are a group of drugs that can change a person's perception, so that they see or hear things that are distorted or that don't exist. They include:

- Psilocybin, found in certain mushrooms called 'magic mushrooms'
- Mescaline from the peyote cactus
- LSD, also commonly known as 'acid'.

History of the drug

Natural hallucinogens in plants have been used for centuries by various cultures for their mystical and spiritual associations. Today, people pick mushroom plant varieties such as 'gold tops' and then cook them to prepare a liquid, or eat them as they would normal mushrooms. Synthetic psychedelics were developed in the twentieth century, reaching their peak of popularity in the 1960s and early 1970s.

In Australia it is illegal to use, possess or supply any hallucinogenic drug. In NSW, penalties such as large fines and/or imprisonment apply.

Forms of the drug

Some psychedelics occur naturally in plant species, while others are manufactured in laboratories. They vary widely in their origin and chemical composition.

LSD is odourless, white and tasteless. It is usually soaked into squares of absorbent paper, often called blotters, which are regulary decorated with particular images or patterns, and taken orally. Each square represents one dose.

Effects

Psychedelics can produce changes in thought, sense of time and mood. The psychedelic experience, or 'tripping', as it is often called, will vary from person to person. The effects can range from feeling good to an intensely unpleasant experience commonly known as a 'bad trip'.

Bad trips can produce feelings of anxiety, fear or losing control. Other effects are a sense of time passing slowly, feelings of unreality, feelings of separation from the body and an inability to concentrate. Intense sensory experiences, such as brighter colours, and a mixing of the senses, such as the sensation of 'hearing' colours, may also be felt. Both positive and negative feelings may be felt during the same drug experience.

Effects of psychedelics usually begin within half an hour and are at their strongest after 3–5 hours, but may be felt for up to 16 hours.

Chemically, LSD is very similar to the neurotransmitter 'serotonin', and the effect of the drug is to increase sensory information delivery into the brain, thus essentially flooding it with an excess of sensation. Other effects may include loss of concentration and 'out of body' experiences.

Blind subjects who take LSD in experimental situations do not experience any visual illusions at all. 'Hallucinations' are usually warped visual exaggerations of what is actually present, and should be more properly referred to as 'illusions'.

Risks and harms

LSD can cause an abnormally rapid beating of the heart and a rise in blood pressure, and can pose a risk for those with cardiac problems.

Some users experience unpredictable 'flashbacks' where they relive the effects of the drug without actually using it. These can sometimes occur years after the 'trip', but usually take place within the first year of the drug experience.

In the period following tripping that is known as the 'come-down', feelings of depression are common. There is also evidence that existing mental illnesses such as psychosis, depression and anxiety can be triggered or made very much worse by LSD.

Fatalities or accidents can occur as a result of 'tripping' in unsafe environments, as a result of people believing they have physical abilities beyond that of normal humans. Reports of people believing that they can fly are not unheard of and people under the effects of psychedelic drugs can be in added danger if in high places, such as bridges or balconies, and can also come to harm if near water.

People should never take LSD or other psychedelics alone, and, ideally, one person should always remain 'straight' to deal with any problems that may arise.

Collecting and consuming wild 'magic mushrooms' can also be risky, as there is a high risk of even the most experienced users accidentally eating a poisonous toadstool or mushroom.

Dependency

Psychedelics are rarely used daily or regularly, but when they are, tolerance (resistance) develops quickly. By developing a higher tolerance, the drug user needs to take larger quantities in order to feel the same effect as before.

Some regular users may develop a psychological dependence.

Withdrawal

There do not appear to be physical symptoms associated with withdrawal from psychedelics.

When to call an ambulance

If the user is experiencing heart palpitations, shortness of breath, wheezing, convulsions, blurred vision or collapses into unconsciousness after taking LSD or another psychedelic.

If the user has passed out or becomes unable to speak or move. If they are still breathing and have a pulse, lie them on their side while waiting for the ambulance.

If the user has no pulse and is not breathing, commence CPR immediately and wait for the ambulance. If the user has a pulse but is NOT BREATHING, commence mouth-to-mouth resuscitation ONLY.

STEROIDS

Steroids are also known as anabolic steroids, roids, gear or juice.

History of the drug

Anabolic Androgenic Steroids (AAS) are sex hormones produced in large quantities in males and in smaller quantities in females. Testosterone is responsible for the masculinising or androgenic effect. It is these tissue-building effects (anabolic) we see as part of natural muscle and masculine development in adolescent and adult males.

In 1935 scientists discovered the primary male hormone 'testosterone'. They then began to explore the effects of supplementing testosterone in men with low testosterone levels and in women with breast conditions and cancers to improve their quality of life. AAS are used to treat medical conditions such as osteoporosis (fragile bones in women), and hypogonadism (small genitals) in men.

In the 1950s, many weight-lifters began using AAS to increase muscle bulk and intensify training. By the 1960s this use was widespread in many sports. People using anabolic steroids include competitive athletes, those concerned with body image, bodybuilders, occupational users such as security guards, construction workers, as well as adolescents—typically young males attempting to reach the same physical stature or athletic performance portrayed in popular media. This has led to the development of testing for drugs in many sports, particularly when played at an elite level. In 1988, well-known Canadian athlete Ben Johnson was stripped of his Olympic gold medal for testing positive to AAS.

Forms of the drug

AAS are available in various strengths as tablets, or as a liquid for injecting. Some of the most common types are:

- Injectable Human Steroids (Deca-durabolin®, Sustanon 250®, Primobolan depot®)
- Injectable Veterinary Steroids (Drive®, Stanazol®, Banrot®)
- Oral tablets (Anapolan 50®, Andriol®, Primobolan tablets®).

As well as the legitimate steroids, there are a number of counterfeit steroids on the black market. Many of these have few (if any) active ingredients. Most of the steroids that body-builders take are synthetic compounds based on the structure of testosterone.

Effects

AAS bind to specific receptor sites in muscles and other parts of the body. These receptors then trigger a range of effects, depending on the cell type, arising from molecular reactions. The amount of tissue-building and male characteristics (e.g. beard growth) that occurs as a result of taking these drugs is dependent on many different factors. These include gender, genetic characteristics, exercise, age and diet.

During the first few days of taking AAS, water retention can take place, which may sometimes add two or three kilos to the body's weight.

Each user will have their own pattern of use, but common features are:

- **Cycling**—steroids are used for a set period of time, followed by a period of no use. Many users vary the dose they administer within each cycle.
- **Stacking**—when two or more different anabolic steroids are combined and used.

Risks and harms

Use by adolescents carries a high risk of permanent damage to bones and tissue, resulting in permanent short stature. Psychological impairment such as increased aggression and irritability, inability to deal with frustration, mood swings and depression can occur. 'Roid Rage' is a term that may be used to describe the aggressive behaviour of some AAS users. While there is no accepted description of this phenomenon, it may represent the extreme end of some users' natural aggression. It is possible to become dependent on anabolic steroids.

Insulin is alleged to have the same effects as AAS, despite no scientific evidence to support the belief that insulin actually increases muscle bulk. Serious dangers are associated with its use and several insulin-related deaths have been reported in Australia among the body-building community.

Human Growth Hormone acts on carbohydrates, fats and protein. This drug can cause serious growth problems including overgrowth of hands and feet and face (acromegaly), pathological growth of the heart, and joint pain.

Amphetamines and ephedrine may be combined and used by body-builders for a stimulant effect during training, or as an aid when reducing body fat.

Clenbuterol, thyroxine and diuretics may also be combined for fat-reducing. There is very little knowledge of the effects of these drug combinations. In many cases, the use of these drugs without proper medical supervision, when combined with AAS, may be life-threatening.

If a person in your family is using AAS and becomes aggressive or violent, look after yourself and other family members as an urgent priority. Their actions may be unpredictable and irrational—even towards those they love. If necessary, seek help from the police, social services or others, or remove yourself or the AAS user from the situation.

Dependency

Tolerance develops with continued use. While there is little evidence of physical dependence developing, many users become psychologically dependent because the drug has given them a particular body type—something that is very important for their self-image. Users can feel afraid of stopping their steroid intake in case that body should change.

Overdose

Steroid overdose can cause collapse, coma, convulsions and death.

Withdrawal

If you wish to withdraw from steroids, specialist advice will be needed depending on the particular steroid and quantity used. Phone the Alcohol and Drug Information line in your state for more information.

Detox and treatment

Oestrogen antagonists, 'proviron' and 'human chorionic gonadotrophin' may be used to manage side-effects, such as gynaecomastia and shrinking testicles.

When to call an ambulance

- If the user is experiencing heart palpitations, shortness of breath, convulsions, blurred vision or collapses into unconsciousness after taking steroids.
- If the user has passed out or becomes unable to speak or move.
- If they are still breathing and have a pulse, lie them on their side while waiting for the ambulance.
- If the user has no pulse and is not breathing, commence CPR immediately and wait for the ambulance. If the user has a pulse but is NOT BREATHING, commence mouth-to-mouth resuscitation ONLY.

METHADONE

Methadone is a synthetic substance produced in a laboratory. It is a depressant drug that slows brain or central-nervous-system activity and belongs to the same chemical family of drugs as heroin—the opioids or narcotic analgesics.

History of the drug

Methadone was first used as a treatment for heroin depend-ence in 1964 and was subsequently introduced into Australia for the same purpose in 1969.

National guidelines for methadone treatment were first endorsed in 1985 by the Ministerial Council on Drug Strategy. In 1993, the Commonwealth, state and territory governments developed a National Methadone Policy which has assisted in establishing a common set of principles for providing methadone treatment in Australia.

Methadone is used to help stabilise opioid-dependent people, enabling them to break the routines and habits associated with their heroin use, become abstinent, or reduce their opioid use. Research studies have shown that methadone improves the health of most opioid-dependent people who choose to enter treatment.

Methadone is legal and is a pure drug. It is longer-lasting than other opioids, such as morphine and heroin, with a single dose usually having effectiveness for 24 hours or longer. This lengthy effectiveness enables it to be used less frequently than other opioids. Methadone is taken orally, making it cleaner and safer than injecting street drugs. Methadone is cheap and can be dispensed in hospitals, clinics or community pharmacies.

Forms of the drug

When given in a treatment program, methadone is generally provided as a syrup which is swallowed. In methadone-maintenance programs, an oral methadone syrup preparation is substituted for the user's usual heroin or other opioid.

Clients are given a dose of methadone every day. The size of the dose is prescribed by a doctor and determined according to the characteristics of each individual. It is worked out so that the amount of methadone given to the user will stop them going into withdrawal for 24 hours, but will not give them the effect of being 'stoned'. Normal activities and functions can, generally, be maintained.

Today's flexible approach to dosage levels means that the doctor prescribes the dose according to the client's needs, rather than having to abide by fixed program rules determining the maximum dose level. The initial daily dose is 20–40 mg, usually taken as a single dose. It can take from several days to some weeks for the new client to be stabilised on methadone. During this time, the dose is gradually increased as tolerance develops, with the person's symptoms and signs carefully monitored until an ideal maintenance dose level is achieved. The client is then usually maintained on a single daily oral dose at this level, without further increases unless other circumstances change.

Some people do well on daily doses as low as 20–30 mg, but most are maintained in the 50–120 mg range. Research suggests that clients receiving daily doses greater than 60 mg are more likely to remain in treatment and to reduce or eliminate their use of illicit drugs.

Effects

Depending on the amount taken, the person's experience, the size of the dose and the frequency with which it is taken, effects and how long they will last differs for each person. It is not unusual to experience one or more of the following: sweating, constipation, lowered sex drive, aching muscles and joints, and itchy skin. Other effects like suppression of appetite, stomach pain, nausea and vomiting can occur and can usually be reduced by adjusting the dose.

Methadone can make some people put on weight, probably due to fluid retention and changes in diet. For men, methadone can lead to delayed ejaculation, particularly in higher doses.

Some women report reduced libido or disrupted menstrual cycles, while some find their cycles return to normal after irregularities that developed while using heroin and other opiates. Tooth decay may be a problem, but regular cleaning of teeth, rinsing, and chewing sugar-free gum can help to counteract this.

Risks and harms

The following side-effects should not generally occur but should be reported to a doctor if they do:

- sedation
- relief of pain
- insensitivity to pain
- light-headedness or dizziness
- narrowing of the pupils
- impaired night vision
- shallow breathing.

When taken in its pure form and in regular doses as part of a treatment program, methadone generally has no severe long-term effects on health.

Dependency

Although methadone is used to help combat other types of drug addiction, dependency is still an issue. Even while dependent on methadone, without the pressures associated with illegal drug use, users are likely to manage their lives more effectively. The longer patients remain in treatment the less likely they are to use illicit opiates, the fewer crimes they commit, the more likely they are to be employed and the less likely they are to be receiving government assistance and to suffer from serious medical conditions. Slow withdrawal from methadone may be accomplished safely and with minimal discomfort when the situation is appropriate for the individual.

Overdose

Methadone overdose can be fatal. Like heroin, methadone is a powerful drug. If a person accidentally uses more than their prescribed dose it is vital that they alert medical and/or clinical staff and then follow any advice given to them.

The main risk of methadone overdose is of stopping breathing. Feelings of extreme tiredness leading to a loss of consciousness and coma occurs (where the person cannot be roused), often with a sudden collapse. Oral methadone can be slow acting and an overdose may not occur until 3–24 hours after taking the dose.

The use of other drugs with methadone can also cause fatal overdose. Other depressants such as alcohol, benzodiazepines (Valium, Serepax, etc.), other narcotics and cannabis interact with methadone, causing drowsiness, unconsciousness, failure to breathe and, ultimately, death.

Some drugs also reduce the effectiveness of methadone or change its effects. On the other hand, methadone can change the effectiveness of other drugs, or produce unexpected side-effects. It is very important for people to let their doctor, dentist or pharmacist know that they are taking methadone, so that nothing is prescribed which could affect the treatment, and so that other medical procedures are safe.

Withdrawal

Slow withdrawal from methadone may be accomplished safely and with minimal discomfort. Without the pressures associated with illegal drug use, people tend to manage their lives more effectively. The longer patients remain in treatment, the less likely they are to use illicit opiates or to suffer from serious medical conditions, the fewer crimes they commit, the more likely they are to be employed, and the less likely they are to be receiving government assistance.

When a person wishes to come off methadone, their dose is gradually reduced, in consultation with their prescribing doctor, over 3–12 months or longer, depending on the size of their regular dosage and the individual concerned. During withdrawal, clients receive assistance and support from their prescribing doctor and other health workers.

Sudden discontinuation of methadone treatment does cause withdrawal symptoms and is not usually recommended. Such symptoms vary and usually begin between one and three days after the last dose. They can include uneasiness, yawning, tears, diarrhoea, abdominal cramps, goose-bumps, a runny nose and a craving for the drug. They typically reach a peak on the sixth day and then last up to one week after that. A feeling of lethargy can last for a while longer.

There are some new methodone-to-abstinence programs. For information contact your state Alcohol and Drug Information Service.

Methadone and pregnancy

Pregnant women who receive methadone treatment are likely to have fewer complications during their pregnancy and childbirth than pregnant women who continue to use illicit opioids. Starting methadone treatment early in the pregnancy reduces the likelihood of complications occurring. Like all opioids, though, methadone does cross the placenta to the unborn child. Babies born to methadone-dependent mothers may go through withdrawal at birth, although with lower doses this is rare. If it does occur it can be successfully treated while the baby is still in hospital.

Methadone also passes to a baby, in very small quantities, through the mother's breast milk. Women may breastfeed safely while on the methadone program if on a low to moderate dose. No immediate ill-effects have been noticed in the breast-fed children of methadone treatment clients, although little is known about the long-term effects on a baby who has had regular doses of methadone in the early stages of development.

Methadone and the law

In Australia, methadone can only be used legally for specific medical purposes approved by the relevant state or territory health authority.

Each state and territory in Australia has different laws about drugs. Under the *Commonwealth Customs Act* of 1901 the importation of methadone is illegal and carries penalties of up to $100 000 and/or life imprisonment. There are no restrictions on the amount of methadone that an individual can have in their possession, provided that it is legally prescribed to them by a suitably authorised medical practitioner.

The laws about the possession, use and prescription of methadone vary from state to state. Those planning to travel interstate should find out what the laws are in the states they are due to visit, and what health services are available. Special arrangements need to be made by people on the methadone program who wish to travel. People travelling to another town or state for a short period of time may request temporary transfer to a pharmacy or program in the place they are visiting. If a client is moving for a longer period, or permanently, he or she will need to make arrangements through their current treatment program to be admitted to a methadone program near their new home.

Overseas travel may be difficult for people on methadone treatment. Special arrangements should be made to conform with regulations of the Commonwealth Department of Health and Ageing and the Australian Customs Service. Certain conditions will be applied, depending on the client's situation. It is extremely important that these are adhered to, as possession of methadone is a serious offence in some countries. The methadone provider should be able to assist with travel arrangements.

When to call an ambulance

If the person is breathing and has a pulse, lie them on their side and dial 000 for an ambulance immediately.

If breathing stops and a pulse can be felt, dial 000 and commence mouth-to-mouth resuscitation (if a pulse is evident, do not attempt CPR).

If no pulse or breathing is evident, dial 000 immediately and then commence CPR.

OTHER PHARMACOTHERAPIES

Pharmacotherapy is the name given to several chemical detox and substitute medication maintenance methods that have been trialled in Australia in the past couple of years, mainly for people who are dependent on opiates. They include:

- Naltrexone
- Buprenorphine, marketed as Subutex® and commonly referred to as 'Bupe'
- Levo-Alpha-Acetyl-Methadol also known as LAAM
- Slow Release Oral Morphine (SROM).

Naltrexone acts to block the effects of opiates (heroin) in the body while the other medications act as an opiate sub- stitute in the body and prevent the person from experiencing withdrawal symptoms. They are trialled as an alternative treatment to methadone.

Naltrexone has been used in Australia and overseas. It is used in two quite different ways: for rapid detoxification and, after detoxification, to support abstinence. It is still controversial and more research evidence is needed as to its efficiency.

Although **naltrexone rapid detoxification or implants** are a popular idea, clinical trials suggest that—like all detox procedures—rapid detoxification is only the beginning of a process. Dr James Bell, who conducted the Sydney Hospital pilot study, says, 'This is not the magic bullet. Being drug-free is a change in consciousness.' While acting on the physical craving it does not stop the emotional or psychological cravings. If you are considering naltrexone as a treatment you need to get reputable specialist advice.

Buprenorphine is a long-acting opioid medication used as a pain reliever, and has been extensively used in France as a maintenance therapy in more than 50 000 patients for over seven years. After a large trial coordinated by NDARC in Australia it has been available for use here since 2001. Overall research shows that substitution treatment with buprenorphine works as well as methadone; people will simply prefer one medication or the other and, due to individual differences, one may be more effective for some people than the other. Some people feel more alert on commencing and during buprenorphine use than on methadone. Buprenorphine has similar side-effects to methadone, but generally they are mild and settle down after the first week of treatment. When starting treatment or during dose increases, patients should not drive or operate machinery until stabilised on their dose. It is dangerous to mix buprenorphine with other drugs such as alcohol, benzos or methadone. Injecting buprenorphine is dangerous and may cause vein damage, ulceration, infection and major health problems. Patients should carry identification that they are taking buprenorphine and advise doctors of the fact, as in hospital or in emergencies, opiate painkillers will be ineffective.

Withdrawal from buprenorphine usually causes fewer symptoms and for a shorter period than from other opioids, but should be done slowly from maintenance doses and with adequate support. Remember that once detoxed, tolerance to opiates soon returns to zero. There have been several reports of people overdosing when they use heroin following detox or ceasing maintenance treatment. Buprenorphine on its own is relatively safe in overdose, but if mixed with other drugs and alcohol it can be deadly.

LAAM is a synthetic opioid with very similar effects to methadone as an opioid substitution drug. It has been trialled in South Australia and Victoria but is unlikely to be marketed, as there is concern that although it has been extensively used overseas, there is evidence of a very small risk of significant side-effects.

SROM is an opioid analgesic. Small trials of its use have been inconclusive. There have been suggestions to use another opioid, hydromorphone, for maintenance, but no trials have been conducted and neither medication can be legally prescribed as maintenance therapy.

SUBOXONE (**Buprenorphine-naloxone**) comes in a tablet form and is designed to dissolve under the tongue. It takes from 2 to 10 minutes to dissolve and the full effect will occur in 30 to 60 minutes. Suboxone is useful in reducing the risks of substitution medication being diverted.

David, 32, was Damien Trimingham's best friend and had been using heroin and other drugs, on and off, since he was in his late teens. David spoke at Damien's funeral. Sadly David passed away from an overdose some time after he spoke these words. David was intelligent and had a kind and beautiful soul. His words here are so true and a fitting way to end the book.

My message would be—don't. If your friends do something, don't follow them. If you have any questions or you feel upset, always try to share your feelings with someone. Don't close yourself off. I think that's what makes people vulnerable to taking drugs, from my experience. With my son, I guess I will just try to set a good example and always be interested in him. You should always love each other. I can't predict the future and what my reaction might be, but I'd like to think that if I see anything happen with drugs in his life I'll try to be non-judgemental and just help him.

Thanks to Paul Dillon from the National Drug and Alcohol Research Centre for his help in producing this information

Knowledge Is Power, Support Is Critical:

contacts and further information

Throughout this book, I have written, with almost a nagging insistence, that knowledge is power. I have also written about the importance of being emotionally supported in order to enable you to support the drug user in your life. The information included in this chapter—some recommended reading and a list of services and support groups across the country that provide good information and that all-important compassion and understanding—is not meant to be a definitive list of what does exist in this country. What it is, though, is a great starting point for anyone who needs to find out more about what it is to be a drug user, what that means for the other people in the life of the drug user, and how best to help yourself in order to help them. Some phone numbers have changed since this book was printed but it is worth looking up the organisations as they still may be running their services.

The first edition of this resource, *A Guide to Coping*, was published in 1998 and we appreciate the assistance of the NSW and Australian governments to Family Drug Support to provide this resource to families. It is now in its fourth edition and is regularly updated. Support is available at helplines such as the 24-hour FDS phone line and by attending FDS Family and Carer Support Meetings or other groups such as Twelve-Step meetings in your area. For some people, individual or family therapy can also be useful.

No matter what your worries, take some time to look after your physical, emotional and spiritual wellbeing.

CONTACTS

National

Alcoholics Anonymous Australia—
    www.alcoholicsanonymous.com.au
Australian Drug Foundation—1300 858 584;
    www.adf.org.au
Australian Drug Information Network (ADIN)
    —www.adin.com.au
Australian Injecting and Illicit Drug Users' League (AIVL)—
    (02) 6279 1600; www.aivl.org.au
Family Drug Support—1300 368 186; www.fds.org.au
Hepatitis Australia—1300 437 222; www.hepatitisaustralia.
    com.au

Kids Helpline (National)—1800 551 800; www.kidshelp.
   com.au

Lifeline—13 11 14; www.lifeline.org.au

Nar-Anon—www.naranon.com.au

National Cannabis Prevention and Information Centre
   (NCPIC)—1800 304 050; ncpic.org.au

Youth Drug Support—www.yds.org.au

ACT

ADIS (Alcohol and Drug Info Service)—(02) 6205 4545

Parentline—(02) 6278 3833

New South Wales

Alcohol and Drug Info Service (ADIS)—(02) 9361 8000;
   outside metro area—1800 422 599; www.druginfo.nsw.
   gov.au

Al Anon—(02) 9279 3600; www.al-anon.alateen.org/australia

Carers Australia—1800 242 636; www.carersaustralia.
   com.au

Drugs and Alcohol Multicultural Education Centre
   (DAMEC) —(02) 9699 3552

Hepatitis C Council of NSW Info/Support Line—1800 803
   990

Nar-Anon— (02) 9418 8728

NSW Users and Aids Association (NUAA)—(02) 8354 7300;
   outside metro area—1800 644 413; www.nuaa.org.au

Parentline—132 055

Northern Territory

Alcohol and Drug Info Service (ADIS)—1800 131 350; Darwin
   (08) 8922 8399; Alice Springs (08) 8951 7580

AIDS and Hepatitis C Council—(08) 8941 1711; outside metro
   area—1800 880 899; www.ntahc.org.au

Queensland

Alcohol and Drug Info Service (ADIS)—callers within Qld—
1800 177 833; www.health.qld.gov.au

Hepatitis C Council of QLD—1800 648 491; www.hepatitisc.
asn.au

Parentline—1300 301 300

Queensland Injectors Health Network (QUIHN)—
(07) 3620 8111; www.quihn.org.au

South Australia

Alcohol and Drug Info Service (ADIS)—1300 131 340;
www.dasc.sa.gov.au

Family Drug Support—(08) 8384 4314; 0401 732 129

Hepatitis C Council of SA—(08) 8362 8443; outside metro
area—1300 437 222; www.hepccouncilsa.asn.au

Nar-Anon—(08) 8272 8228

South Australia Voice for IV Education (SAVIVE)—
(08) 8334 1699

Parentline—1300 364 100

Tasmania

Alcohol and Drug Info Service (ADIS)—1800 811 994;
www.turningpoint.org.au

HIV & Hepatitis C Info/Support Line—1800 005 900

Parentline—1300 808 178

Victoria

DirectLine (Victorian Drug Services)—1800 888 236

Family Drug Help—1300 660 068; www.familydrughelp.
org.au

Hepatitis C Council of Victoria—(03) 9380 4644; outside
metro area—1800 703 003; www.hepcvic.org.au

Parentline— 13 22 89

VIVAIDS—(03) 9329 1500

Western Australia

Alcohol and Drug Info Service (ADIS)—(08) 9442 5000; outside metro area—1800 198 024; www.dao.health. wa.gov.au

Hepatitis Council WA—(08) 9328 8538; outside metro area— 1800 800 070; www.hepatitiswa.com.au

Parent Drug Info Service—(08) 9442 5050; outside metro area—1800 653 203; www.dao.health.wa.gov.au

Parentline—(08) 9272 1466

West Australian Substance Users Association (WASUA)— (08) 9321 2877; www.wasna.com.au

READING LIST

Adaptation

Bradshaw, J. 1992, *Home Coming*, Bantam, New York

Anger

Lerner, H. 1995, *The Dance of Anger*, Harper Percival, New York, USA

Taris, C. 1989, *Anger: The misunderstood emotion*, Simon & Schuster, London

Cannabis

National Drug and Alcohol Research Centre, *Quitting Cannabis*, available at http://ndarc.med.unsw.edu.au/NDARCWeb. nsf/resources/Resources_pdfs/$file/cannabisfinal.pdf, accessed 1 September 2008

Drug Users' Lives

Davies, L. 1997, *Candy*, Allen & Unwin, Sydney

Families and Drugs

Bloomfield, H. 1985, *Making Peace with Your Parents*, Bantam, New York

Clark, I. 1999, *Saving Jessie*, Doubleday, Sydney

Goodyer, P. 1998, *Kids and Drugs*, Allen & Unwin, Sydney

Fear

Jampolsky, G. 1985, *Love is Letting Go of Fear*, Bantam, New York

Jeffers, S. 1987, *Feel the Fear and Do it Anyway!*, Fawcett Columbine, New York

Grief

Bechek, E. 1973, *The Denial of Death*, Simon & Schuster, New York

Levine, S. 2005, *Who Dies?*, Gateway Books, Nevada City

Harm Reduction and Treatment

Denning, P., Little, J. and Glickman, A. 2004, *Over the Influence*, Guildford Press, New York

Heroin

Krivanek, J.A. 1988, *Heroin Myths and Reality*, Allen & Unwin, Sydney

van den Boogert, K. and Davidoff, N. 1999, *Heroin Crisis*, Bookman Press, Melbourne

Inspiration

Gibran, K. 1952, *The Prophet*, Alfred A. Knopf, New York

Williams, M. 1922, *The Velveteen Rabbit*, Doubleday, New York

Methadone

Byrne, A. 1995, *Methadone in the Treatment of Narcotic Addiction*, Tosca Press, Australia

Motivational Interviewing

Miller, W.R. and Rollnick, S. 2002, *Motivational Interviewing: Preparing people for change*, Guildford Press, New York

Over-Responsibility

Goldbloom, S. 1998, *The Book of Rachel*, Allen & Unwin, Sydney

Personal Growth

Moore, T. 1992, *Care of the Soul*, Harper Perennial, New York
Scott Peck, M. 1978, *The Road Less Travelled*, Arrow, New York

Relationships

Jensen, D. and Newman, M. 1998, *Really Relating*, Random House, Sydney

Self-Esteem

Dyer, W. 1976, *Your Erroneous Zones*, HarperCollins, New York
Satir, V. 1976, *Making Contact*, Celestial Arts, Berkeley

War on Drugs

Gray, M. 1998, *Drug Crazy*, Random House, Sydney
Manderson, D. 1993, *From Mr Sin to Mr Big*, Oxford University Press, Melbourne